ADVANCE P

CHANGE TACTICS

"A generous, powerful handbook for practitioners. April Mills has created a book you'll want to share, but your copy will be too marked up to let out of your sight."

—Seth Godin
Author of *This is Marketing*

"The world needs your best ideas. But becoming a change agent isn't always easy. April Mills' invaluable new book shows you exactly how to navigate obstacles and overcome the status quo to make a difference."

—Dorie Clark
Author of *Reinventing You* and executive education faculty,
Duke University Fuqua School of Business

"A poster on our walls at Menlo Innovations says: Technology changes quickly, people change slowly. In her book, *Change Tactics - 50 Ways Change Agents Boldly Escape the Status Quo*, April K. Mills has set about changing that status quo formula with a simple, yet powerful idea: **Embrace Change!** This isn't about learning to accept change, or trying to get along with change, but literally giving change a big bear hug and moving forward with change as a lifelong friend, not a mortal enemy. And, so as to not leave you wondering how, she delivers fifty practical techniques for doing just that. You need this book ... now!"

—Richard Sheridan
CEO & Chief Storyteller, Menlo Innovations
Author of *Joy, Inc. - How We Built a Workplace People Love* and
*Chief Joy Officer - How Great Leaders Elevate Human Energy and
Eliminate Fear*

"The world continues to move faster and faster. Many organizations invest a lot of time in defining strategy, but very little in the actual strategy execution. Most leaders in organizations have never been properly equipped to truly lead change. In *Change Tactics*, April Mills gives readers real tools to help leaders understand how to drive change."

—Kathy Gersch
Chief Commercial Officer, Kotter International

"In the Pixar movie *Ratatouille*, chef Gusteau makes the radical claim that "Anyone can cook," but like a good chef, he keeps his recipes secret. In her first book, April Mills made the radical claim "Anyone can be a change agent." With this book, she shares her recipes."

—Paul Klipp
Executive Agile Coach at Wawel Hill
and Co-Host of the Agile Book Club Podcast

"Today's most agile, innovative organizations recognize the need to embrace change and transformation. With April's insights and expertise to guide you on this journey, you'll be equipped with the tools, tips, tricks, and techniques to empower yourself and your organization on the journey. Where so-called change experts provide platitudes and pontification about transformation in theory, April puts the concepts into practice with real-world experience gained over years of advocacy and hard work to deliver business results. This book will change how you view your role as a change agent in your organization in ways that will make you a more effective leader."

—Monique Hayward
President & CEO, Nouveau Connoisseurs Corporation

"Status quo is the thing that stops us and our organizations from reaching their full potential. To battle it, you need help. This is where April's book comes in. With her extensive experience as a successful change agent, April created an impressive collection of powerful tactics to battle status quo. This is what you need when you hope to transform!"

—Aga Szóstek
Author of *The Umami Strategy: Stand out by Mixing Business with Experience Design*

"Anyone leading change or wanting to make change happen should read this book. April provides practical tips to not only make change more impactful, but to speed up the process and keep you motivated along the way. Organizational change is a process and this book is your guide."

—Amanda Gibson
Organizational Growth & Innovation Strategist

"Right at the start April reminds us that finding good business books isn't the problem, it's that we don't take action. Hamlet said that overthinking a problem, the biggest bane of change management in my experience, is what causes "enterprise of great pitch and moment...to lose the name of action." The book is clearly born of the reality of having to move an organization through change, while not having a lot of time to theorize on it. So, design rather than plan, remember it's not about you, and take action...pick up the book!"

—J. Kendall Lott
CEO and President, M Powered Strategies

"April has an incredible talent for conveying approaches to change that are practical, actionable, and apply no matter how big the change is or what change you're trying to make. Wherever you are in your change journey, this book provides just-in-time tactics to create a sustainable, people-centered transition to achieve even the seemingly impossible."

—Rhea Stadick
Organizational Transformation Advisor
and co-founder of Future of Work PDX

"I secretly hope that April adds two more tactics to the 50 that are currently in this book, then makes a deck of cards. I'd carry the deck with me so that whenever I got stuck, I could shuffle it, deal the cards out one by one, until I'm unstuck. Brilliantly helpful."

—Clarke Ching
Author of *The Bottleneck Rules* and *CorkScrew Solutions*

"Keep *Change Tactics* on your most easily accessible bookshelf. Whatever challenge you face—change stalled, people ignoring you, trapped in "red tape," budget stuck—there's a change tactic for that. I said, "Doh! Oh no, I do this!" You will too. Better change tactics; start now! "

—Liz Lockhart
Sr. Director of Project Management and Training at Smarsh,
Instructor of Operations Leadership at the Pamplin School of Business,
University of Portland

CHANGE TACTICS

50 Ways Change Agents
Boldly Escape the Status Quo

Gabe—
Keep driving change!

April K. Mills

APRIL K. MILLS

ILLUSTRATED BY SARAH MOYLE

CHANGE TACTICS:
50 WAYS CHANGE AGENTS BOLDLY ESCAPE THE STATUS QUO

Copyright © 2021 by April K. Mills

Licensed pdf copies of this book are available for non-profit organizations by emailing april@engine-for-change.com, Subject: Non-Profit Book Offer. Please include the formal name of the non-profit in the email. Thank you for giving your best to good causes. God bless you.

Published by: Engine-for-Change Press
Ellensburg, Washington, contact@engine-for-change.com

Edited by Sue Vander Hook
Designed by Phillip Gessert
Indexed by Maria Sosnowski

ISBN: 9781736862704

BUSINESS & ECONOMICS/Leadership

Dedicated to Joseph Bradley

TABLE OF
CONTENTS

FOREWORD

You never change things by fighting the existing reality.
To change something,
build a new model that makes the existing model obsolete.

—Buckminster Fuller

In my view, there are two key realities we have all been required to acknowledge in the early part of the 2020s: change is happening faster than ever before, and we're all in this together. Change is happening faster than ever before, and it is our job as people to drive it. We the people are in this together, and it is in all of our best interests to drive change *for* the people rather than driving the people to change.

I lead both Change Projects and Training at Smarsh, a software-as-a-service company headquartered in Portland, Oregon. It is my job to both lead teams and directly drive change throughout the global 800+ person organization in a way that is human-centric and achieves our strategic business outcomes.

In the past, "implementing change" has looked like announcement emails, all staff meeting presentations, IM channel notifications, executive messaging with little follow-up, posters, smoke signals and simply relying on hope. This is the status quo. What I've learned through these experiences is that this does not work. April Mills knows we can do better, and she is ready to share 50 better ways or Change Tactics to help your change initiatives be successful in the right way—finally escaping the status quo and moving towards a new normal.

I was first made aware of April through a conversation with a student of mine, and a colleague of April's. In a coaching conversation with my student, he shared about April and how she drives change and inspires others to drive change at scale thoughtfully and in a human-centered way. Seeing how this extremely smart, PhD turn MBA student described April's knowledge, skills, and abilities, I was immediately intrigued, and little did I know, I was about to be delighted. Within a week, April was in my home office virtually through an educational event with Agile PDX where she shared the concepts of *Everyone is a Change Agent*. I was both overwhelmed by the coincidence and extremely engaged. I knew I needed to learn more from April—as much as I could.

April has a unique approach towards change and interacting with individuals and teams at all levels. In *Everyone is a Change Agent* she shared how to drive change, not people and to utilize various organizational elements to make the right things easy. *Everyone is a Change Agent* up-leveled the way I approach change initiatives and it is required reading for each aspiring Project Manager on my team. A personal note, in the time that I began to implement April's Change Agent Essentials, I achieved a promotion in my job and rose to a new level of leadership.

Building upon the foundations set forth in April's first book, *Change Tactics* is the field guide every change leader needs not only to have on the shelf and remember a few concepts from, but to **use actively and share.**

Why I love this book:

1. April is right; we can do better. We must do better.
2. So often we run too fast to pay attention to the impact we have on people
3. The better way is not always the fastest way, but it is the most effective
4. Each tactic is practical and easy to understand, even for the non-change leader.

If you wish to drive change effectively, you need this book. You need April's insight and mindset to escape the status quo. April is a truly empathetic leader who drives change in the right way. You want to learn from April. Similar to most of life's most difficult challenges, this is up to you to embrace. It is up to you to decide you want to escape the status quo and move towards better, more impactful change.

Drive change, not people, use the tactics, and escape the status quo to the point that others wonder how you learned to be so effective and influential. I want to see this reality for you.

—Liz Lockhart
Sr. Director of Project Management & Training at Smarsh
Adjunct Instructor at the Pamplin School of Business,
University of Portland

ACKNOWLEDGMENTS

Friends, family, partners, supporters, and encouragers. I have so many people to thank.

Mike Doyle, my coach, who encouraged me to finish this book in spite of—and because of—the pandemic.

Dear friends and colleagues who reviewed the many drafts: Joseph Bradley, Dilek Ciplak, Kresta Desposato, Jan Dhaenens, Amanda Gibson, Dean Goodmanson, Mandy Hackett, Karen Holt, Steve Holt, Rona Kisilevitz, Stephanie Liefeld, Liz Lockhart, Kendall Lott, Jaye Matthews, Vikki Mueller Espinosa, Sean Murphy, Ryan Olson, Antara Prasad, Steve Remsen, John Roberts, Hilbert Robinson, Rhea Stadick, Aga Szóstek, Rex Williams, Autumn Witherspoon, and Marta Zoglman.

My outstanding publishing team: Sue Vander Hook, copy editing; Phillip Gessert, design; and Maria Sosnowski, indexing.

Sarah Moyle, my phenomenal illustrator who celebrates five years of this change and publishing journey with me.

Michelle Berenz, graphic designer, Engine-for-Change Press logo creator and dear friend.

Liz Lockhart for her wonderful Foreword and encouragement through-out the project.

The early pre-order supporters who earned and deserve *big thanks*: Matt D'Elia, Marissa Eyon, Russ Field, Chelsea Grace, Nick Hammer, Bing Hu, David Mendies, and Kristy Sand.

Joi and David Rubino for letting me write in their basement to keep up my pace.

Joe Bradley for being 1 in 10,000 who started me on this amazing journey and supported me always.

All those who wrote blurbs and reviews to spread the word about *Change Tactics*.

Matt and our four wonderful kids: Helen, Ted, Alice, and Henry. They always support me, especially on those weekends and evenings when I had to say, "Not now. I'm writing."

My friend and colleague, Steve Remsen, once told me a saying:

Everyone has one book in them;
only when you've written two books can you call yourself
an author.

Thank you, *Change Tactics* readers, for making me an author by encouraging me to bring this book to life. I'm continually grateful to be on your change journeys with you.

"For I know the plans I have for you," says the Lord.
"They are plans for good and not for disaster, to give you a future
and a hope."
—Jeremiah 29:11

God bless you!
April K. Mills
april@engine-for-change.com

Ellensburg, Washington
May 2021

INTRODUCTION

If your goal is to make change,
it's foolish to try to change the worldview of the majority
if the majority is focused on maintaining the status quo.
The opportunity is to carve out a new tribe,
to find the rabble-rousers and change lovers
who are seeking new leadership
and run with them instead.

—Seth Godin, Tribes

Some stories haunt you. This is one of those stories.

In November 2006, Joseph Bradley was attending the Theory of Constraints International Certification Organization conference in Miami, Florida.

One afternoon, Bradley wasn't resting between conference sessions. He was outside in the muggy Miami heat looking for Eli Goldratt, the father of theory of constraints and the conference's star attendee.

Bradley had a burning question to ask Goldratt.

He found Goldratt sitting alone on a bench, indulging in his classic between-session habit: smoking.

While Goldratt relaxed with his pipe, Bradley asked his question:

> You've written all these books. As far as I can see, you have given us, the readers, detailed roadmaps to success. Here's what I don't understand. Why are you giving away all your secrets for the price of a book?

Goldratt smiled.

Bradley continued.

> If you read the book, you can translate it to action and get results similar to the book. Why don't people just do that?

Goldratt calmly answered:

> Less than 1% understand that the books are roadmaps to action.

Bradley:

> I didn't realize that.

Goldratt:

> Think about it.

Bradley:

Yeah, I guess you're right.

Goldratt:

Now, of those who understand it is a roadmap, less than 1% of them actually take it and do something.

Bradley:

That's 1 in 10,000!

Goldratt:

Yes. You've done the math correctly.

1 in 10,000!

1 in 10,000!

1 in 10,000!

Those odds—and that story—have haunted me for years.

How could so few people use such powerful tactics? How could we improve the odds of implementation, not just the theory of constraints but any change?

Seeking the answers to those questions has propelled me for the past 14 years and led to this moment when you are reading a book filled with powerful tactics you can use today, a book that—I hope—sparks you to escape those 1 in 10,000 odds.

To escape those odds, I propose we do three things. I'll do two steps, and you can focus on one vital step.

1. I will replace your old foundation for change with a powerful new foundation.
2. I will provide you 50 ways to escape the status quo through easy-to-implement change tactics built on the powerful new foundation for change.
3. You must act and actually change tactics. Only when you act will you become part of the still rare but growing number of outstanding change agents.

**This isn't a book to be merely owned,
but one to be read and
—most importantly—
to be lived.**

So with that bold gauntlet thrown down, let's begin.

REPLACE THE OLD FOUNDATION WITH A POWERFUL NEW FOUNDATION

Status quo—the existing state of affairs. So says Merriam-Webster.

My dear friend and colleague John Roberts defines status quo as **the cultural library of how things get done here.**

The status quo is so reinforced and so embedded in muscle memory that it not only blinds us to alternatives but often to its very structure. Like the fish doesn't notice the water; we don't notice the foundation of how we create change.

The status quo for creating change is a foundation of using force to compel others to change. I call this **Driving People.**

With Driving People as the foundational status quo, our change results are dismal.

In 2018, Gartner published some sad change statistics. According to Gartner's report, "Managing Organizational Change":

- 50% of changes were clear failures
- 16% had mixed results
- only 34% were clear successes

Some people hope that these superficial tweaks will create better change results; issue your demand with a smile or catchy video and tagline; wait to threaten until after people have had time to comply; tell them the change can be self-directed, even though you still intend to dictate what self-directed means for them. These tweaks haven't produced better results. We need something more.

Most of the suffering we experience in these change-filled times is self-inflicted. It isn't *what* the change is but *how* we do it that hurts. To shift the *how*, we need a new foundation for change.

We build this new foundation when we choose a change for ourselves and clear the obstacles for others to choose it too. I call that **Driving Change**.

Driving Change isn't just an alternative to Driving People; it is a repudiation of it.

You cannot both Drive People and Drive Change. You must choose, and that choice makes all the difference in your change success and sustainability.

When you're Driving Change, you see potential where others see the impossible.

When you're Driving Change, you've found the antidote to change saturation as your personal, organizational, and community change capacity grows, and grows, and grows.

When you're Driving Change, you're active—even proactive—in contrast to Driving People, and that causes many to be passive and reactive.

Change is not just something special. Everything is a change.

A change is a difference you are determined to make, whether as an individual or as part of a group or organization.

Change—a name I prefer to more commonly used terms such as *project* or *initiative*—is any effort undertaken with the goal of innovating a solution, meeting a need, or otherwise improving the world.

It is the delta between what is and who you imagine you could be.

A change is, however simple or complex, your effort to make the world a better place.

—April K. Mills, *Everyone Is a Change Agent*

There are many books that discuss change and purport to map a better path to results. Few books challenge the status quo foundation of change—Driving People. Even fewer suggest a defined, powerful alternative such as Driving Change. And even fewer books actually tackle Goldratt's 1% of 1% observation and provide a deliberate, detailed call to action through specified, easy-to-implement change tactics.

I've long been a student of those who see the gap and are trying to close it. In 2010, John Kotter, a world expert in leading change and author of *Buy-In*, wrote:

> The challenge is that the amount of thought and education put into creating good ideas is far higher today than the knowledge and instruction on how to implement those ideas. In the world of business, for example, the field of strategy has made huge advances in the past twenty years. The field of strategy implementation, in contrast, has made much less progress.

That same year, Kotter visited me and the Guiding Coalition I led for seven years based on Kotter's 8-Step Model. Kotter said:

> Only 15 percent of all organizations are really trying to understand how to live with and respond to the rate of change. Of the organizations, 15 percent are trying to move in a direction that they know works, 14 of the 15 percent are struggling because of the culture or environment that drives them. Only 1 percent of the organizations in the world are making progress; they are doing what you all are doing.

For more than a decade, I've been living at the leading edge of change and building foundations, essentials, and tactics to help you become more than 1 in 10,000 and to see your changes succeed.

If we don't close the gap between the changes we want and the foundations and tactics we use to achieve the changes, we will perpetuate what so many have today: **change suffering.**

Change suffering is the physical, emotional, and spiritual pain experienced during poorly implemented changes.

Most people just want terrible changes to go away so their suffering can end. But if your life, organization, or community needs the change, we must do more than give up or create more suffering. We must change our tactics.

I love change. I love the dynamic hope that springs forth from someone who can both imagine a better future and bring it into existence. And I am motivated to prevent as much change suffering as possible.

This book is a testament to my motivation. Why else would a wife, mother of four, and full-time employee pour my nights and weekends into a book like this? I have studied at the feet of many change thought leaders and had countless opportunities to practice and refine change tactics. I'm now well qualified to bring forth change tactics you can use to close the 1 in 10,000 gap, improve your odds of change success, and reduce your suffering while increasing joy. If this book can remove even a small portion of change suffering from the world, I will consider my time well invested and myself truly blessed.

CHANGE TACTICS DEFINED AND OUTLINED

I've spent more than a decade cultivating, curating, and creating change tactics to cover many common change situations you'll face.

I've built the tactics to be easy for a novice to try yet powerful enough to help even in the toughest change situations. By practicing these change tactics, your confidence in your change agent skills should grow. You deserve to be confident. Remember, there are multitudes that won't even read a book like this, so you're already in a rare club. You can be proud of that.

These change tactics attack practical problems that can only be solved by action.

But what action?

When trapped in the status quo, it is hard to see alternatives.

In this book, you'll find 50 alternatives—50 ways change agents like you can escape the status quo and achieve change.

This is not about stopping anyone else from doing anything. This is about starting something different for yourself.

Each tactic is a short vignette that starts with these four topics:

1. A goal—what are we seeking
2. A status quo tactic—our traditional default action and the thinking behind it
3. A change tactic—a fresh way based on Driving Change.
4. A why—the motive for taking any action and the change tactic specifically

Then I detail and discuss the status quo tactic and change tactic.

Most tactics include a checklist, a worksheet, or hints to help you apply the change tactic quickly.

A lot of the tactics include a personal story of how I or others have applied the tactics and what results we got.

Many of the stories or analogies mention the challenges and status quo of implementing Agile in organizations. I've spent the last six years immersed in the world of Agile, and examples of its challenges quickly spring to mind. Agile (with a capital A) is a method once used for software development but now applied to a range of project and program management situations where "work is divided into a series of short tasks, with regular breaks to review the work and adapt the plans" (Oxford Learners Dictionary). If you don't have Agile experience, don't worry. Replace Agile in the story with the change you've experienced, and I bet the story will still hold power for you.

Speaking of replacing one story with another, throughout the book I use a concept I call **Change Algebra** where I describe some change stories using variables to substitute for specific people, changes, and organizations. Person X, who works for Organization Y, encountered Obstacle A when creating Change B.

Using Change Algebra allows me to show you the universality of change situations, to reduce situations to their simplest form, to protect those who would rather not have their story told exactly, and to allow you to fill in your specific scenario to imagine the tactics in action.

When you've finished reading through the 50 change tactics, you'll recognize the status quo all around you and some opportunities to change tactics.

To keep the book direct and actionable, I've intentionally stated the tactics directly without citations and footnotes. That keeps the tactics brief and practical.

As you've already seen in this introduction, sometimes explaining the change tactics and new foundations for change requires some custom terms. You'll find those terms marked in **bold** when I define them. I also included their definitions in the glossary.

MOVE FROM KNOWLEDGE TO ACTION

You can use these change tactics anywhere. If people are present and you need change, these change tactics will work.

I've tested the tactics in a range of industries and organizations. I've applied them in government, community, corporate, consulting, information technology (IT), human resources (HR), and engineering situations. I've applied them to local, regional, and global change.

You don't have to act on the change tactics all at once. You don't even have to read the book all at once.

Skim it. Try one change tactic. Then try another.

Read the conclusion.

Browse the Appendices, especially Appendix 1 if you haven't read my book *Everyone Is a Change Agent* and are unfamiliar with the Change Agent Essentials. You don't have to read the book in order to understand *Change Tactics*, but it will certainly help you have a deeper, richer experience. The books aren't a series, but they go together.

Not all the change tactics will resonate with you. Think of the 50 change tactics in this book like 50 flavors of ice cream. Some are very different, and some are subtle differences on a common theme—like an ice cream shop offering plain vanilla, vanilla bean, and French vanilla.

Chances are that a few of the change tactics will speak to your immediate situation. And over time, you can revisit the tactics as new challenges pop up. Keep this book handy as a reference you can go to whenever you feel stuck or in need of an energy boost.

You can start small, but start today. The change tactics that are safe to try are designed to allow you to begin slowly without jumping from novice to expert overnight.

You'll find tactics in here that you already do. Wonderful! You'll find tactics in here that you've never considered. Fantastic!

To track your action, you can score yourself on your use of the change tactics by recording a + for the change tactics you've done and a—for those where you're still stuck in the status quo.

Now we're ready! Let's beat those 1 in 10,000 odds together.

CHANGE TACTICS SCORECARD

Tactic	Title	+/-
1	Shift from Forcing to Influencing	
2	Control Your Change	
3	Break Free from the Power Paradox	
4	Replace Certainty with Humbleness	
5	Tell Your Story	
6	Tell Stories about Today	
7	Cultivate Followers at a Distance	
8	Absence Makes the Heart Grow Fonder	
9	Let Them Feel It	
10	Sort the Active from the Passive	
11	Practice Wound Care	
12	Let the Conscripts Leave	
13	Check for Clarity	
14	From Consensus to Commitment	
15	From Helpless to Empowered	
16	Find Your Hidden Change Agents	
17	Study the Hometown Prophets	
18	Build a Team Full of Superheroes	
19	Shine a Light on the Invisible People	
20	Create Your Relay Team	

Tactic	Title	+/-
21	Say Their Names	
22	Pile Up the Partnerships	
23	Build a Tower of Support	
24	Heat Up the Teacup	
25	Shrink the Change	
26	Give It a Title (Not a Name)	
27	Create a Different Future	
28	Speed Up the Pace	
29	From Change Waterfall to Change Agility	
30	A Healthy Dose of Change Design	
31	Design for the Early Majority	
32	Design for Joy	
33	Sketch the System	
34	Calibrate the Change to the Half-Lives	
35	Make the First Step Easy	
36	Scale the Change	
37	Make Stone Soup	
38	From Consumption to Renewal	
39	Create Your Opportunities	
40	Feel the Momentum	
41	Eliminate the Trivial	
42	From Events to Daily Moments	

Tactic	Title	+/-
43	Move the Results into the Meeting	
44	Don't Stall Behind No	
45	Clear the Traffic Jam	
46	Write a New Rule	
47	Choose Your Mirror	
48	While You Were Away	
49	Measure the To:With Ratio	
50	Assess Trust	

CHANGE TACTICS
FOR YOU

1
SHIFT FROM FORCING TO INFLUENCING

There is no limit to the extent my influence can grow,
the same cannot be said of my ability
to control anyone but myself.

—Anonymous

Goal—Create sustainable change

Status Quo Tactic—Show up to force the change

Change Tactic—Show up to influence the change

Why—Because force fades, but influence sustains

Status Quo Tactic – We assume we must force a change, and people assume we will force them to change. This is Driving People in action.

When we believe in Driving People, we focus on opportunities to force people to change. We create elaborate plans to direct how they must change. We send e-mails to large distribution lists telling them what they must do (or else).

Sometimes they comply; often they don't.

Then we demand that others force the change. We think up ways to punish people who don't change, and sometime we actually follow through on the punishments. Usually, we plan the punishments but never deliver them.

Once we force the change, we know we can't stop. When we don't get the progress we want, we find more places to push. The time devoted to forcing the change grows and grows. The moment we let up on the pushing, the demanding, and the punishing, people assume we don't care anymore, and if they were changing at all, they stop. So we keep forcing until we're exhausted, and the people are exhausted too.

To make room for new changes and all the time and energy to force them, we must stop forcing the old change. Our time between demands grows, and attention to the change wanes. Ultimately, when the change fails, we agree with those who say we didn't pay enough attention to the change.

Sometimes we create local, distributed change enforcers—regional quality managers, team Agile coaches, conscripted change champions—who force the change in our absence. They, too, will grow weary, and when they do, the change dies.

Once upon a time, we heard of a change that wasn't forced—a change that spread and sustained. We assumed that leader must have found some magic. It wasn't magic; it was a switch to Driving Change.

• • •

Change Tactics – We assume we should influence the change. People are ready to follow someone who's willing to clear their obstacles so change is easy to follow. This is Driving Change in action.

When we believe in Driving Change, we look for opportunities to influence the change, first by our example and then by removing the obstacles that block others from also choosing the change. We look for opportunities to share our excitement and hear their concerns. We create and tell stories that spread.

Sometimes they are reluctant to follow, and often they're excited and rush to join us.

Then we keep role modeling the change, clearing the obstacles of others, and sharing how easy it is for them to join us. We spend time with people, clearing obstacles and driving toward results and sustainment. We get to spend our time planning celebrations.

Once we influence the change, we won't want to stop. When we get progress, we'll know where our influence is resonating and see novel ways to amplify it. Our time devoted to the change will shrink as other change agents that follow step forward to drive the change and influence others. We'll know when our influence is sustaining when we can focus on a recent change and the momentum of our first change doesn't slow down. People will keep moving forward on the change, and their energy will keep growing.

As we move on to fresh changes and also Drive Change on the recent changes, the spreading example of leading through influencing and clearing obstacles will spread. Talk of this as our new normal begins.

Local change champions will reveal themselves, network, and connect. They'll energize each other and you too.

Once upon a time, we heard of a change that had to be forced, a change that struggled and died. We'll assume that leader must have never learned they could change tactics. We'll ensure all our colleagues and friends know they can always Drive Change, and we'll never again Drive People.

• • •

We find the proof that force fades but influence sustains in the contrast between the change-forcing leaders whose names we forget quickly and the lasting power of the great leaders of organizational lore who are long departed but never forgotten, such as Admiral H. G. Rickover and Andy Grove.

I've been lucky enough to work in both the U.S. Navy's nuclear power program and Intel Corporation. Still today, decades after Rickover and Grove departed—their influence encourages people to drive for new achievements. Both men, tough as they were on those they led, never expected anyone to do a change they weren't willing to do first. And they dedicated their lives to clearing the obstacles that stood between their organizations and greatness. That's Driving Change.

PRACTICE GUIDE TO SWITCH FROM FORCING TO INFLUENCING

Switching from forcing (Driving People) to influencing (Driving Change) requires practice. It is a lot like learning to ride a backward bicycle.

What's a backward bicycle?

A backward bicycle has the handlebars turned in the opposite direction of the front wheel. You can see the backward bicycle and the practice needed to ride it in this eight-minute video:

https://tinyurl.com/Bike-Backwards

Practice often. Create for yourself daily and weekly opportunities to Drive Change, act on the change, and clear an obstacle for someone else to join you. Without practice, you won't get better.

Switch your plan to switch your actions. Assess your change plan for tasks where you are forcing others, and switch the tasks to things you can do or obstacles you can remove for others.

Create places to practice.

- Meetings
- Online forums

- Communication channels
- Work evolutions
- Training sessions

Practice with others. Reach out to the people who need to change. Ask them to join you and practice Driving Change too.

When you fall, try again, and again, and again. There's 49 more tactics here to help you keep practicing.

2
CONTROL YOUR CHANGE

I will do what I can, with what I have, where I am.

—The Change Agent's Motto from Everyone Is a Change Agent

Goal—Control your change plan
Status Quo Tactic—Plan for others to act
Change Tactic—Plan for us to act
Why—Because the control rests with the one who acts

Status Quo Tactic—You have a change plan, but you aren't in control of your change.

Look at your change plan.

How many of the actions are for others to do?

How many of the actions in your plan are your tasks? (Telling them to obey doesn't count.)

If the number of tasks you're doing is less than the number of tasks that others must do, then you aren't in control of your change. They are.

And when they don't complete your tasks, what will you do?

Tell on them to a higher manager? Wait? Hope?

Or try something else?

• • •

Change Tactic—You are in control of your change plan because you've filled it with actions you can take with what you have and where you are.

This is a change plan built on the **Change Agent's Motto:**

I will do what I can, with what I have, where I am.

When you've built your change plan on the Change Agent's Motto, you control the destiny of your change.

It will require you to break free of all the standard change plan tasks—tell them, train them, remind them, tell on them, punish them, shame them, and start again.

A change plan that's in your control includes tasks such as these:

- Clarify terms for ourselves, and confirm the clarity with others.
- Set a **Concrete Goal,** and then share it to learn if it also resonates with others.
  <Who> will <experience> <what> <where> <when>.

- Alter the processes (or just write them down) to drive alignment in your thinking, and then seek alignment with others.
- Clean up obstacles that stand in your way and inhibit others. If you don't know what the obstacles are, you can ask them. They'll happily tell you.

When your change plan focuses on controlling what you can and helping others join you to speed it up, you'll see yourself and others move from objects of change to managers of change to potent change agents.

• • •

As a pet project, I worked in fits and starts over eight years to force the U.S. Navy to open a childcare center for civilians to use on the base in Bremerton, Washington. I kept trying to find the right person to force change, but it didn't matter how many times I wrote a plan for the change, they would not do it just because I said they should.

Then, as I discovered and built the theory and practices of Driving Change instead of Driving People and used the Change Agent's Motto and the other Change Agent Essentials, I realized I had been controlling the change incorrectly. I flipped from focusing on forcing others to act to doing what I could, with what I had, where I was. And that change in tactics made all the difference.

An amazing team of women and Executive Director Rick Tift and I controlled our change, built great partnerships, and achieved our Concrete Goal—a childcare center on base available for civilians. Where I'd failed for eight years, we succeeded in three. In February 2012, we cut the ribbon on the childcare center, a monument to the power of change tactics.

CONTROL CHECK

Score your change plan.

+1 for each task you control

−1 for each task that demands someone outside your team do something

Rework your plan until you're above zero.

Bonus: A perfect score is a plan with only +1 tasks.

3
BREAK FREE FROM THE POWER PARADOX

We assume that others are powerful and we are weak.
The truth is that others are less powerful than we think they are,
and we are more powerful than we have imagined.
This is the Power Paradox.

—April K. Mills

Goal—Leverage power to achieve change

Status Quo Tactic—Assume that others are powerful
and we are powerless

Change Tactic—Leverage our power and appreciate
others' limitations

Why—Because when we're free of the Power Paradox,
we're free to achieve our change

Status Quo Tactic—Everywhere, the **Power Paradox** ensnares.

> We assume that others are powerful and we are weak.
> The truth is that others are less powerful than we think they are,
> and we are more powerful than we have imagined.

People lead their changes and their lives assuming that others have so much power and they have so little power.

We take these assumptions of who does and doesn't have power for granted and never test them. We feebly take our changes to the people we think have power and beg them to support us.

How many weeks or months did you spend trying to get that executive to sponsor your change?

Well...

Or if your change was executive-directed, how many weeks or months did you spend crafting the perfect plan for the executive to bless it with their authority only to find out that no one in the organization cares if that executive sponsors something because even the people who report to that executive don't comply with their orders?

Yeah...

Did you ever pursue a promotion thinking that when you made the next level of leadership, suddenly you'd have the genuine power to make change happen? Did you get the promotion? Did you get the power? How many individual contributors have missed the true powerlessness in most first-line and middle manager positions in modern organizations until they became a first-line manager themselves?

So many.

There is no magical step on the ladder that conveys enough power to Drive People. I've met senators, admirals, and CEOs who claimed they lacked the power to implement their changes. Maybe the issue isn't how much power we have but how much we think we have and what we do with it.

• • •

Change Tactic—If you think you aren't powerful, you will prove yourself right. And the opposite is true. If you look for your own power, you will find it everywhere.

If you aren't a senator, you can't offer legislation on the floor of the Senate Chamber and vote to pass it, but you can create the language for a bill and work with a senator to influence other senators to vote for it.

If you aren't the CEO, you can't set company strategy, but you can partner with the CEO on parts of the CEO's strategy that you believe in and work to make it succeed in your area and spread your example from there.

The elegant escape from the Power Paradox is to discover and leverage your own power and help others discover and leverage theirs too. If you don't know where to look to discover your power, look back to the Change Agent's Motto:

I will do what I can, with what I have, where I am.

When you list all the things you can do and the things you have and the unique place in space, time, and history you inhabit, you'll see how richly powerful you really are.

And you can help others do that too.

Partner with people in other positions who have unique authority to help make the changes you want to make. Help a mid-level leader see that even though they don't have $10 million and 100 people to put to work on the change, they have their 10-person team and their $500 discretionary budget, and there is a lot they can do with that. Help a new employee see that they possess a rare gem—a fresh perspective—in an established, market-leading company. That's rare and powerful.

• • •

In 2011, when Bremerton Beyond Accessible Play had just begun the effort to build Kitsap County's first accessible playground, everyone assumed the project would be easy if we could just secure an appropriation from our powerful congressman. I was the organization's president, so others encouraged me to meet with the congressman's staffer to discuss the process. I thought I knew how little power I had and how much power the congressman had.

In the meeting with the staffer, I learned of new limitations on the congressman's power. And in accepting that limitation, I found our power as we strategized how, given the Change Agent's Motto, we would do what we could do, with what we had, where we were to raise more than $500,000 as fast as possible on our own.

Over the next three-and-a-half years, faster than anyone thought we could, Bremerton Beyond Accessible Play raised more than $500,000 from large grants, charity group donations, individual contributions, a pancake breakfast, a silent auction, and change collection jars at local gas stations and businesses. We would take every nickel and penny people would donate.

Free of the Power Paradox, we accepted the limits on the power of others and worked hard to get the most out of the power we did have. We achieved amazing results. In September 2014, the over 9,000 square foot beyond accessible playground opened at Evergreen Rotary Park in Bremerton, Washington. It has been a marque playground for the region ever since and a beautiful place where all may play.

You can see the playground by visiting Evergreen Rotary Park in Bremerton, Washington, or watching this video that was recorded at the playground's grand opening. https://tinyurl.com/SoAllMayPlay

POWER PARADOX FREEDOM WORKSHEET

The key to this tactic is to look for all the ways you can put what you have—position, connection, resources, smarts, influence, knowledge—to work for your change and how you can help others see all the capabilities they have to bring to bear on the change.

Start by listing five things you can do with the power you have.

1. _____
2. _____
3. _____
4. _____
5. _____

Honor the limits of others by listing five things you assume another leader could do that maybe they cannot.

1. _____
2. _____
3. _____
4. _____
5. _____

Then check with them and ask, "Do you really have this power or not?"

It will help you calibrate what you can really do together. Chances are good that they are assuming they have much less power than they actually do.

Once you are free of the Power Paradox and living the Change Agent's Motto, you can continue to do this exercise and free others from the Power Paradox.

Freeing them from the Power Paradox may be one of the greatest gifts you can give them after introducing them to the concept of Driving Change, not people.

4
REPLACE CERTAINTY WITH HUMBLENESS

The best laid schemes o' Mice an' Men
Gang aft a-gley,

An' lea'e us naught but grief an' pain,
For promis'd joy!

—*Robert Burns, To a Mouse*

Goal—Move confidently forward

Status Quo Tactic—Invest in the plan

Change Tactic—Map the terrain, and humbly learn your way forward

Why—To move fast while respecting that the future will differ from the plan

Status Quo Tactic—Burns wrote his poem about "best laid schemes o' Mice an' Men" going awry in 1785, but it seems we haven't remembered the lesson because we still encourage most change managers to put their hopes in perfecting their change plans.

In 1871, Helmuth von Moltke reminded us that "no plan of operations extends with any certainty beyond the first contact with the main hostile force." Perhaps we shouldn't equate the audiences for our changes with "the main hostile force," but we often treat them like they are—like people we must subdue to our intentions versus lead to their better success.

Ask yourself these two questions:

1. How long did we invest in planning our last change?
2. After we started implementing it, how long did we follow the plan before changing it?

There's an odd habit that follows this status quo tactic of trying to build the plan—the tendency to spend weeks or months building that plan and then spending more months creating the presentation of the plan for senior leaders who will give you only one-hundredth of that time you've invested before they pass judgment on your change plan.

I bet you've had executives direct you to reconsider earlier assumptions or tactics that you had already assessed and dismissed. That happened because the executive's thinking is closer to where you started than where you ended up after months of deliberation. This misalignment and the weight of senior authority results in the plan being reset to the executive's maturity on the issue, not the team's maturity. I've seen teams implode from the frustration of this reset. There are few things worse than compelling a person to spend months of their precious life to build a plan only to have it thrown out after a 20-minute presentation.

If the plan passes through the executives, the typical call to action for executives is for them to role model the change in order to drive action. I fully support role modeling (as I already covered in Tactic 1—Shift from Forcing to Influencing) as a key piece of Driving Change, but the role modeling called for here is better labeled **playacting**—when an executive only superficially invests in getting the task done versus actually committing to the change.

Playacting—You've observed playacting if you've ever seen an executive presentation on a change that sounds wonderful but bursts over the audience like a pin-pricked water balloon when an audience member asks a simple, probing question and the executive shows they have only memorized the talking points and not internalized what role modeling the change really means.

An executive-approved plan is more brittle than a change leader's personal obsession with the change plan. Why? Because each piece of additional information, transformational or trivial, that prompts a change in plan requires a rebriefing for executive approval. No one can move forward quickly under these conditions. These delays are totally self-inflicted by the change leaders and the executives. We've built the change so we can move only as fast as the executives allow the plan to adapt versus at the rate of our learning. That is hopelessly wasteful of both time and potential.

• • •

Change Tactic – We aren't lacking for paths we could take. What we must have is the humbleness of leaders to admit at the beginning that they aren't certain (and can't be certain) of what will work. Experience grants us greater but not absolute certainty.

If you were absolutely certain before you acted, I would challenge you:

> Why didn't you act months or years ago when you may have been less certain but your situation (e.g., market opportunity, energy to apply to the change, technological lead) was better?

Whether you're in business or in a nonprofit, by the time anything is certain, you've lost your competitive advantage or people have needlessly suffered while you waited to be sure.

When you are Driving Change, you can admit what you don't know but show how you are trying to learn it. Then keep learning your way forward with safe experimentation.

Experimenting is not the same as flailing about looking for anything that works. If you don't know what is around that next bend in the change, don't commit everyone to charge in that direction. Send a few people to experiment in that direction (i.e., with a new tool, in a new partnership), and quickly get their report back. What's their experience after one week or two? Scouting ahead is a tradition of multiple disciplines over millennia. Trust it.

The scouts should map the terrain ahead. Mapping the terrain involves two key steps: checking for settlers and declaring your boundaries.

Settlers are the people who do the job of your change today (current settlers), the people who used to do it (past settlers), the people who think they should do it (missing settlers), and the people who benefit from you doing it (downstream settlers).

Look for them. When you've found them, learn from them, invite them to join you, and celebrate them. Never ignore them.

Declaring your boundaries means describing to yourself and others interacting with your change what your scope and limits are. If you're focused on Agile in your department, say so. Don't claim (or allow others to claim) that you are driving a broader continuous improvement effort for the corporation.

If you do these two things, you can chart a path that is easier to understand and joined by those currently outside of your change. Most conflict in change efforts comes from people outside the change that are unclear of your boundaries or your actions toward settlers, and then they interfere with your change based on their misunderstandings.

Acceleration Note: If you're ready to eliminate any executive approval step for any change plan, then jump ahead to Tactic 50—Assess Trust.

• • •

When I first implemented this tactic, it shocked me how well it worked. In years past, the time from the launch of an initiative to its first win was typically three to four months because the teams spent all those months planning and budgeting for the future they wanted to create. That was what every other team before them had done, so we didn't think of it as a delay of results but just the way things work.

Then we implemented this tactic. We got our first win two weeks after the initiative launch. And we hadn't applied this tactic on only one team; we switched 20 teams simultaneously. It felt like the universe had rocketed forward.

So you don't have to start small, but you have to start. Pick one team or 20 and move forward today.

MAP YOUR BOUNDARIES WORKSHEET

Who are your settlers?

Current:

Past:

Missing:

Downstream:

What are your boundaries?[1]

Your Concrete Goal typically reveals your boundaries, and you can add more detail.

<Who> will <experience> <what> <where> <when>

Physical boundaries:

In this division but not the entire organization; in this town but not this county

Time boundaries:

Focusing on this project or starting a series of projects

Process boundaries:

This process or all processes

What will you do to scout out the terrain and learn your way forward?

Talk to ... learn ... connect ... try ...

---

1. For more on Concrete Goals or mapping your boundaries, see Appendix 1 or Chapters 7 and 8 of *Everyone Is a Change Agent.*

TELL YOUR STORY

*I don't think a leader can accomplish major change without
being willing to slice yourself open and become part of the change.*

—*Mimi Silbert, quoted in Change or Die by Alan Deutschman*

Goal—Win people to follow you

Status Quo Tactic—Keep the focus on your authority to
force them to change

Change Tactic—Share a personal story about why this
change matters to you

Why—Because people follow leaders who are with
them, not against them

Status Quo Tactic—In many changes, the executive is little more than a barker of orders, the figurehead on the auditorium stage, or the picture in the masthead of an e-mail. The executive rarely does more than lend their name and position to the change. We put executives in this position when we believe we must have an executive to make the change happen. Our status quo thinking goes like this: without the executive's authority to Drive People to change, they won't change.

We compound this tendency to lead with authority to force others to change when we focus our communications on what people must do— the orders or policies—versus stories about the change and what the leader will or won't be doing because of this change. This focus on the orders they must obey causes changes to appear cold and calculated, not something personally important to the executive.

• • •

Change Tactic—Every change leader, executive or not, should share a personal story of how they're adapting to the change and will be role modeling Driving Change, gathering followers, and building trust simultaneously. When you tell them how you realized this change was vital or how you identified and overcame an obstacle to adopting the change, you are helping them join you on this change journey.

The goal of each story is a demonstration to the team that you trust them enough to be authentic and vulnerable with them. You want the stories to be ones they can tell others so the power of your authenticity can spread. Through the spread of the stories, you will build confidence in you and your commitment to the change.

If you don't have a story related to your change, then your first task is to do something that is worthy of a sharable story. Use the Tell Your Story template below to organize your thoughts. The size of the obstacle you've overcome is irrelevant, so choose a small, easy-to-overcome obstacle. The key is not your victory over the obstacle but your willingness to admit you have had to change to make this successful.

•••

Here's a simple example story to get you thinking about what you might do. As you read it, think about whether you would be more likely to follow his lead in the project after hearing his story.

Hi. My name is Vijay. I'm honored to join this team.

As an expert in Process Y, when I first asked to join this team, I realized I should learn a lot more about Topic X so I could catch up to all you've already done and show up ready to take part.

I spent the last week studying a lot on my own, and yesterday I reached out to Marta and Autumn to answer my biggest questions.

Thanks to both of them for sharing their knowledge with me.

I look forward to learning more from all of you as I bring my background in Process Y to this project.

With this simple story about his efforts during the past week, Vijay has shown the team that:

- He has expertise and wants to share it.
- He is on the team because he wants to be.
- He's willing to do the work to learn and keep up.
- He shows his gratitude.
- He is ready to work.

Would you want Vijay on your team? I would. Would you be willing to follow him as he shared his Process Y experience? I would. I bet you would too.

You can be like Vijay. Just tell your story.

TELL YOUR STORY TEMPLATE

What was the change?

What were your obstacles to accomplishing the change?

What action(s) did you take to overcome the obstacle(s)?

What about the story will make it memorable and sharable for others?

Bonus: Who can you name and celebrate for helping you overcome the obstacle(s)?

Where can you share this story first?

Where will you continue sharing this story or tell another story?

6
TELL STORIES ABOUT TODAY

Yesterday is history, tomorrow is a mystery, and today is a gift...
that's why they call it the present.

—attributed to Eleanor Roosevelt

Goal—Increase enthusiasm for the change right now

Status Quo Tactic—Make promises about what is coming

Change Tactic—Tell stories about what has happened or is happening today

Why—Seeing is still the fastest path to believing

Status Quo Tactic – Typical change communications are full of promises. Unlike newspapers, communications about change focus on the future instead of the past or the present. We fill status updates more with promises about the future than completed or current events.

> This change will transform this or that next quarter.

> This change will fix the things that have been ailing the organization for the past decade.

> If only we do this one new thing, then next year, after we implement this strategy... Wow!

The promise is always a better future, but there is rarely an action at the moment except vague calls to get ready or get involved, which usually mean encouraging your fellow employees to complete some tasks such as taking a survey or clicking follow on a communications site.

For the more conceptual changes such as improving quality or safety or strengthening or transforming the culture, we offer or are offered even fewer tangible actions. The future may be vivid, but the specifics of what the executive and everyone else must do now are nebulous.

When we're the audience members and not pitching the change, whether we're in auditoriums or conference rooms or logged on to virtual sessions, we experience how our audience is likely reacting to our change. Will you admit you struggle to pay attention to the latest talking head throwing out change buzzwords and flashing polished slides? I will. It's a battle to keep my attention.

This status quo reveals that in many change efforts, the communications carry more weight than they can bear. When we assume that they are the vehicle through which we enact the change, we've overloaded them.

Too many times I've seen change leaders build promises into their messages, assuming the support to fulfill the promises will come once the people were excited about the change. I've never seen that work. Though they were well intentioned, they didn't keep the promise, they broke trust, and scar tissue formed between the leaders pushing the change and the people.

• • •

Change Tactic—If you want to generate momentum through your communications about the change, talk about what you've already done and what is happening today. When you tell stories about what's already happened and what is happening today, it helps people see that the change is really happening, and they feel they will miss out if they don't get involved now.

You can test the power of this tactic by simple comparison. Which would you rather click on to read more?

A. We've already landed five enormous deals. Here's how the new sales process can help you succeed today.
B. A new sales process is launching soon—what you need to know.

When you talk about things that have already happened, people don't have to imagine the change; they can see it. When you mention the names of who already took action, people can connect with the proper role models and change advocates. Show them what is open to them today, and you'll learn who is engaged—who clicked, who signed up, and who got involved.

The existence of results and a path to engagement allow the people you're speaking with to move easily from unaware to attentive to active. Then all you have to do is support them as they invest themselves in creating the outcome you want.

If you need to talk about the future, talk about it as an open set of options (it may include...) versus a closed set of instructions (all should...). That allows your plans to develop without breaking promises.

If you discipline yourself to only talk about what has happened and what is happening today, you will inspire others to have confidence in you, inspire hope in your future, and inspire action today. Even if you say that something is happening next week, tell them what they can do today. And ask them if they did something else to post it and share it so you can learn from it.

You can use the Tell Stories about Today Worksheet to help you craft your change messages.

• • •

Rather than telling a specific story, I want you to pause and think back to the last change you leapt out of your seat for and got involved with right away.

What did you hear, see, or read that gave you the confidence and information to leave what you were doing and join them right away?

How can you recreate those attributes for your change audience so you can trigger that same reaction in them?

TELL STORIES ABOUT TODAY WORKSHEET

To have a story to tell tomorrow, we must do something today.

This worksheet will help in the time before a communication opportunity so you've done something and gathered results to show that you are Driving Change and have something for others.

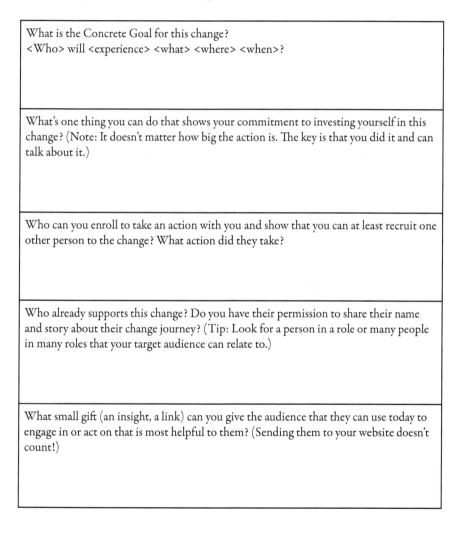

What is the Concrete Goal for this change?
<Who> will <experience> <what> <where> <when>?

What's one thing you can do that shows your commitment to investing yourself in this change? (Note: It doesn't matter how big the action is. The key is that you did it and can talk about it.)

Who can you enroll to take an action with you and show that you can at least recruit one other person to the change? What action did they take?

Who already supports this change? Do you have their permission to share their name and story about their change journey? (Tip: Look for a person in a role or many people in many roles that your target audience can relate to.)

What small gift (an insight, a link) can you give the audience that they can use today to engage in or act on that is most helpful to them? (Sending them to your website doesn't count!)

Who or what can you leave with them to support them in becoming an advocate for the change today?

Do you have an example you can share of a point of resistance or an obstacle that you already found and have overcome? (This doesn't have to be big. You are noticing obstacles and taking action; it was not a mountain that you moved.)

When and where will you share the story? How will you create multiple impressions from this story?

How will you record and share the story for people who weren't there to hear it or for people who want to share it?

7
CULTIVATE FOLLOWERS
AT A DISTANCE

It's said that actions speak louder than words;
actions speak farther (and further) than words too.

—April K. Mills

Goal—Earn their attention to advance our change

Status Quo Tactic—Interrupt their life when it is convenient for you

Change Tactic—Forge a relationship so they'll interrupt their life for you

Why—Because attention granted is more powerful than attention demanded

Status Quo Tactic—Our world is filled with interruptions—pop-up ads, unsolicited texts, e-mail blasts, and visits from or open forums hosted by executives on their latest change. Each one distracts us from what we were doing to what they want us to see.

We are all guilty of interrupting others to get progress on our change. The question is whether interrupting their lives on our schedule is the best tactic when we want to earn their attention to advance our change.

So much communication in today's world isn't for the audience of the change; it's for the business, the management, or the elected official. If we're involved in the changes the business, management, or officials are pushing, we are helping them spread their messages at the times and cadence best for the change plan, not best for the audience.

So much of today's communication is blasted to the biggest audience possible with the most glitz or polish to trigger the most reaction. And so many are ignored. Imagine all the time you've put into communications in the past that don't get read or into events that get superficial attention. Are those attendees on your online forum really listening?

If you're the audience, are you paying more or less attention while the rate and volume of communications bombarding you increase? What voices are standing out above the cacophony? Chances are good they are following a very different tactic to get your attention.

· · ·

Change Tactic—Start a movement and make it easy for followers to opt in. That honors their time and lets you know who is truly with you (or at least willing to give you a shot to earn their attention).

The best change leaders are the ones you invite into your life, the ones you seek, the ones you want to listen to. Outstanding leaders know it is the audience's interest that moves their message along, not how physically close they are to the audience or how often they break into their audience's lives. Technology can close any physical distance, but only the desire to have a relationship can close the figurative distances between us.

In 1999, Seth Godin coined the term *permission marketing* to differentiate this type of relationship from the status quo, interruption-focused marketing. Twenty-one years later, the status quo for change is still interruption-focused and is suffering the same poor results.

With our entire lives just one stream of interruptions, it is hard for anyone to break through and influence us. Those few have cultivated permission to have our attention.

Many change leaders can quickly cultivate this permission. Here are three keys:

1. Be a role model for the change.
2. Give your audience something, and expect nothing in return.
3. Make it easy for followers to find you and enroll themselves in your change.

The first key is to Drive Change, to live the change you are seeking in others. If you do, you will have plenty of things you can share about the change. You will also have a lot of examples of opportunities you've taken to role model the change for others. From simple actions like starting meetings on time if you're seeking better meetings to announcing a global work stand-down after an accident to prove a commitment to a safety culture, you'll find that people are eager to find leaders they can look up to and emulate. Leading by example works!

The next key to generating global, sustainable permission is to give people something, expecting nothing in return. This gift may be as simple as sharing key information with them that they can only get through you (think of a story from the board meeting that shows the seriousness of the corporate situation) or your unique perspective on the situation that helps them see something in a fresh light. If your first contact with someone is to ask them for something, they won't likely want to hear from you again.

The third key is to let people enroll to stay in touch. *Followers* is a common term on social media platforms, but it is an uncultivated aspect of organizational life. The flawed assumption is that if someone is lower on the hierarchy, they are automatically a follower. The better term for those lower in the hierarchy is *constituents*.

Constituents may be in the region assigned to your authority, but they may or may not be an advocate for you and your leadership position. How do you find out who are merely your constituents and who your followers are? Give them a way to show you which one they are. Leverage an external or internal platform, and ask them to follow you. That's a simple way to see who is nominally with you.

Just because someone gives you a big distribution list of constituents doesn't mean you have those hundreds or thousands of people on your side. Change stalls when the leader lacks followers willing to open their e-mails, connect on social media, attend their events and take action.

• • •

You should use travel to amplify your following and your knowledge of how you can serve your audience, not to assert your authority over them.

In 2019, at a conference in Florida, I finally met Seth Godin in person. We only spoke for a few minutes, but after more than a decade of following him via e-mail, books, and online events, meeting Seth was a pinnacle moment.

Who would say that meeting you is a pinnacle moment for them? What would it mean for your change if they were followers committed enough to see you that way? Imagine what you could change then!

CULTIVATE FOLLOWERS AT A DISTANCE CHECKLIST

What will you do to role model the change?

What will you give your audience and expect nothing in return?

How will you make it easy for followers to find you and enroll themselves in your change?

ABSENCE MAKES THE HEART GROW FONDER

One option is to struggle to be heard
whenever you're in the room...
Another is to be the sort of person who is missed when you're not.
The first involves making noise.
The second involves making a difference.

—*Seth Godin*

Goal—Wisely use your time to Drive Change

Status Quo Tactic—Go to all the meetings you're
invited to

Change Tactic—Only go to the meetings that are
Driving Change with good tactics

Why—There's only one you, so don't waste it

Status Quo Tactic—Many of us are calendar zombies. We go to whatever meetings our colleagues invite us to. We're honored if people want us on their teams. We try to do what we can to help anyone be successful. That is an honorable approach, but it also leaves us time-crunched, and we struggle to advance the changes we care about most.

We admit we can't be our best everywhere all the time. We confess we are using some of those ineffective meetings as protected time to clean out our inbox, or if we have a wireless headset and are working from home, maybe we get the dishes done while barely paying attention to the meeting.

We go to all the meetings because we haven't considered that we can give ourselves permission not to attend everything that is sent our way. What would we do if we granted ourselves that permission?

• • •

Change Tactic—You can and should be selective about what teams you join and what meetings you attend.

To change tactics, you can take the passive path—just stop going, and see if anyone notices. You can decline the meetings on your calendar, not send a notice of your cancellation, and just go about your life with your time back. If you don't show up and no one notices, you'll learn again what you already knew—you weren't putting your best into that change.

If you take the active path and stop going, in a way that helps the team you are leaving succeed more in the future. If you choose the active path, here are some benefits:

1. You get back your time so you can invest in your higher priority activities, but you know you did what you could while you were on the team.
2. You can offer feedback to the team leader about why you are choosing to not take part. If the timing of the meeting is bad for you, say so. If the meeting isn't run well (no agenda, no minutes), share your feedback. If they are Driving People

instead of Driving Change, give them *Everyone Is a Change Agent* and this book to help them succeed.

3. You can offer your spot on the team to another teammate who would benefit from the development of their own change agent skills by helping that struggling team succeed.

Whether you choose the passive or active path, in order to succeed at this tactic, you must overcome an enormous obstacle—your ego. It's hard to think about a world where our lack of presence goes unnoticed or our colleagues accept it, but that is what you may encounter as you leave the team.

• • •

When you're only attending the teams you're committed to adding value to, people will notice. When you send your decline notices for weeks that you are on vacation, you'll get messages back saying, "We'll miss you." And if you're really making a difference, I bet you will hear:

While you were gone, we remembered to ask ourselves,
"How can we Drive Change here?"
And it helped us make more progress.

CALENDAR CHECK

Review your calendar.

List the teams you're on and the recurring meetings you attend for each one.

Decide which ones to stop attending or continue attending and if you will choose to be passive or active.

Then list what action you will take based on your decisions.

Example

Team	Meetings	Stop or Continue	Passive or Active	Action
Quality Initiative	Core team—Mon at 9	Continue	Active	Help set an agenda expectation
	Subteam—Wed at 4	Stop	Active	Let them know the time is bad for me
	Comm team—Tue at 1	Stop	Passive	Stop going for now

Team	Meetings	Stop or Continue	Passive or Active	Action

9

LET THEM FEEL IT

Indeed, if we consider the unblushing promises of reward
and the staggering nature of the rewards promised in the Gospels,
it would seem that Our Lord finds our desires not too strong,
but too weak.
We are half-hearted creatures,
fooling about with drink and sex and ambition
when infinite joy is offered us,
like an ignorant child who wants to go on
making mud pies in a slum
because he cannot imagine what is meant by
the offer of a holiday at the sea.
We are far too easily pleased.

—C. S. Lewis, *Weight of Glory*

Goal—Create transformed people through experience with the change

Status Quo Tactic—Expect transformation out of the same-old situations

Change Tactic—Transform the experience of change

Why—Because it is hard to desire something you've never experienced

Status Quo Tactic—When I ask people in my audiences to raise their hands if they have ever been the victim of someone Driving People and forced to change, nearly all the people raise their hands.

No one is exempt from an experience with terrible change. We may think:

This time it will be different.

Then it never is.

So we can be forgiven for thinking that how change is today is the best it can be. We've learned to settle for Driving People.

But change can be so much better. Like the pride of graduation day, the joy and butterflies of a wedding day, or the bursts of tears and flooding joy of a new baby's arrival, change can feel that way.

In *Heart of Change*, John Kotter provides two lists of emotions, ones that stall change and ones that speed up change.

Emotions That Stall Change	*Emotions That Speed Up Change*
Anger	Faith
False pride	Trust
Pessimism	Optimism
Arrogance	Urgency
Cynicism	Reality-based pride
Panic	Passion
Exhaustion	Excitement
Insecurity	Hope
Anxiety	Enthusiasm

I struggle with nearly all the changes I encounter because I know how much better the change could be. The gap between what is and what could be is so large that it is a void that vacuums energy and enthusiasm into it. The drain of Driving People—how to force these others to change—is exhausting. It assumes the worst and gets the worst. There is a better way.

You will speed up when you build a change on the speed-up emotions. I've experienced it. I've built it. I've scaled it. You can too.

But you can't shift from stalled to speed until you stop Driving People and start Driving Change.

• • •

Change Tactic—When we Drive Change, we tap into what is best in us and our best intentions toward the change and toward others, and then we help unleash that best in others. Only they can offer their best, but we can build the opportunities for them to bring their best forward.

When we build meetings with optional attendees so everyone who is there is someone who wants to be there, we are unleashing powerful, wonderful emotions.

When we thank people for their effort to show up and shine, we are amplifying wonderful emotions.

When we complete a small first step together, we are reinforcing powerful team emotions and are on a roll to even better success and emotions.

It is positively addictive to experience joy in creating change. I wouldn't believe change could be better, feel better, or sustain better if I hadn't experienced it.

It's a transformative moment. You can't go back to not knowing what it feels like. And once you know what it feels like, you want that feeling repeatedly.

These emotions are inherent in you and the others on your change team if you only Drive Change, not people, and allow the emotions in people to surface and channel into change momentum and powerful results.

The crisis in our organizations and our changes today is not the absence of emotion but the suppression of it—put on a cheerful face for the video call. All we need to do is stop telling everyone to change and start choosing the change for ourselves. Let our emotions out to support the change, and then help others choose the change too. You'll feel amazingly different when you *get* to do something instead of *have* to do something.

Let's not be easily pleased. Let's go after joy in our changes by Driving Change together. It will make all the difference!

•••

We can all create that powerful, emotional experience of change for ourselves and others. The Guiding Coalition at Puget Sound Naval Shipyard cured me of ever tolerating standard change again. It helped hundreds of others experience the powerful emotion of positive change, too, and you can experience it today.

You can watch the videos of the 2010 Guiding Coalition delivering their mid-point reviews and listen for the emotion words. You can read the emotion in their voices, on their faces, and in their body language. These are people who are getting to do things they firmly believe in, and they are excited for the extra effort. Passion. Enthusiasm. Amazement. Honor. Joy.

Here's the link to one video (there are more links in Appendix 2) https://tinyurl.com/2010CCI-D-Part1

LET THEM FEEL IT STRATEGIES

- Start the meeting with gratitude. Let people share what or who they are grateful for and why.
- When someone offers to complete an action, amplify their offer with a statement about how and why you have trust and faith in them.
- Celebrate your wins to build reality-based pride.
- End with round-robin sharing of what you're most looking forward to in the following week as it relates to the change.

What other strategies can you think of and try?

CHANGE TACTICS
FOR THEM

10

SORT THE ACTIVE FROM THE PASSIVE

Lead for action, and you just might get it.

—April K. Mills

Goal—Activate the change agents

Status Quo Tactic—Assume that passive people will never be change agents

Change Tactic—Assume that anyone can be an active change agent

Why—Because everyone is a change agent once they believe they can be

Status Quo Tactic—When Driving People is your organization's status quo, you'll find a lot of passive people. They will wait for orders, constantly saying the directions aren't clear enough and demanding certainty before they will move forward. These are learned passive behaviors. Some call these behaviors *playing the victim*. Sadly, they aren't playing. They have been victims, and they've learned these behaviors as a coping mechanism.

Truly wounded organizations begin the long process of trying to eliminate their passive people and hire active people, only to quickly turn the new active people into passive people. My friend and colleague Charles Lambdin (@CGLambdin on Twitter) summarized this practice with a simple tweet:

A: We hire top talent and lay off underperformers.

B: So...your culture is like an underperformer factory?

You'll never activate the passive people by telling them not to be passive. That pushes these people farther away from an active, empowered set of behaviors. You'll have to change tactics if you want to activate your change agents.

• • •

Change Tactic—An active or passive tendency is situational. Just as we can impose passivity, we can cultivate activity. We can be active on one team and passive on another.

Driving People situations trigger passivity in nearly all of us. It feels easier to give in to the force or just give up. It is easier. But easier isn't better for us or for the organization. When we need better, we need to Drive Change to trigger the active part inside us and in others. We can activate others if we know where they are—active or passive—so we can meet them where they are.

You can't simply ask people directly if they are active or passive because even previously active people can slip into passivity without even recognizing it.

It's a gradual process that can creep over any of us, and because it isn't a sought-after condition—especially if we've seen ourselves as active change agents in the past—we will probably be in denial. Hence, a quick assessment of ourselves (or others) in a specific situation can be enlightening. The Active-or-Passive Self-Assessment leads anyone through that personal reflection.

• • •

Years ago, I found myself—a change agency author—in a completely passive state. I had reacted to a toxic work situation by abandoning my agency and allowing myself to be tossed about by the demands of the day. I was—to use a sailing metaphor—without sail and rudderless, adrift. Then I changed teams. In that new situation, I rekindled my active fire for change. It took the contrast to show me just how passive I had become. Leaving the toxic team was a good first step, but it took many more practice steps before I was back in good, active, change-agent shape.

So if you find yourself or anyone else in the passive state, remember that we all can become passive. Give yourself or them grace, and remember, we don't have to stay passive. Our active change agent always remains in us.

ACTIVE-OR-PASSIVE SELF-ASSESSMENT

The purpose of this self-assessment is to determine how active or passive you are in a change. Circle the answer that most reflects your tendency in that situation or environment. Your answer may vary depending on the situation or environment, so answer with a specific context in mind. If you have several contexts to assess (i.e., on your staff, in an initiative team, on a committee), complete the assessment for each setting.

You can use this assessment individually, as teams, or between teams to be transparent about your challenges.

Situation / Environment:

I...

1. Wait for others to set and enforce expectations
2. Comply with expectations once others set them
3. Set my own expectations and rise to any expectations set for me and drive to achieve my expectations

I...

1. Need to be reminded of my tasks
2. Do tasks when assigned
3. Look for opportunities to contribute to the project and complete the tasks quickly

I...

1. Need to be assigned learning and have others track it to completion
2. Complete the learning assigned
3. Seek opportunities to learn and apply what I'm learning before being asked

SCORING

3–5 = Passive Zone

Chances are good that this situation or environment is a forced task for you. You are coping with your lack of interest in the topic or lack of safety to be yourself in the environment by adopting a passive posture.

Get a replacement for the task, or get reassigned. If you have to stay, find something in the task to be excited about. Seek partners to help create safety (physical and psychological) in the situation or environment.

6–7 = Neutral Zone

You aren't passive, but you aren't active either; you're stuck or transitioning from passive to active or from active to passive.

If you're stuck in neutral, you need to practice being active. What's one thing you can safely try by the end of this week?

If you're transitioning from passive to active, keep going. Keep trying new things. Get going. You can do it!

If you're transitioning from active to passive, now is the time to stop your slide before passivity takes over. What aspect of the situation is scoring the lowest? What's one thing you can do to move up one number? Who can you ask to help you? You don't have to do this alone!

8–9 = Active Zone

Consider yourself among the fortunate. Make sure you are sharing the goodness with others, especially those who are in the neutral zone who need help to stop their decline into passivity or could use a boost to get them to the active zone. Keep removing obstacles for others to join you in the active zone!

11
PRACTICE WOUND CARE

The time for the healing of the wounds has come.
The moment to bridge the chasms that divide us has come.
The time to build is upon us.

—Nelson Mandela, Inaugural Address, 1994

Goal—Quickly gain support for the change

Status Quo Tactic—When facing resistance, push harder

Change Tactic—When facing resistance, practice wound care

Why—Because when we heal our change scars, we can go faster on all future changes

Status Quo Tactic—When we need a change to happen, we think the ends justify the means. With the status quo of Driving People, we feel justified in doing everything within our power—threatening or bribing—to get people to change. That justification manifests as suffering to the people being forced to change. We don't hear their concerns. We don't meet their needs. They are told to "figure it out" and pushed and pushed and pushed until eventually we all abandon the change, accept only a portion of what we intended, and declare a false victory or let the change fade silently.

This forcing, pushing, punishing, and cajoling leave the people in the organization suspicious of change, reflexively resistant to any change, and truly wounded and scarred. If we classified organizations like industrial land, we could say that the organization is a brownfield. The United States Environmental Protection Agency (EPA) defines a brownfield as a property, the expansion, redevelopment, or reuse of which is complicated by the presence or potential presence of a hazardous substance, pollutant, or contaminant. Our organizations that are spoiled by Driving People also have open wounds from past changes and hardened change scars.

When leaders recognize the brownfield of change wounds and scars, they look for a new greenfield of new employees in a new business unit in a new location to expedite the change. The EPA warns industries to avoid these greenfields, these previously unpolluted spaces. To me, it seems the EPA sees avoiding cleaning up the brownfield as a dereliction of corporate duty. I do too. Unfortunately, many companies celebrate greenfield stories. Think of the IBM PC success at their Florida spin-off, or Boeing's moving its assembly to South Carolina, or General Motors' NUMMI plant. But even when these greenfield efforts work in their greenfield location, they do nothing to clean up the brownfield they left behind, and they often come at prohibitive costs for most organizations that aren't IBM, Boeing, or General Motors.

So what are most leaders to do?

• • •

Change Tactic—Face squarely that you have scarred employees by driving them to change. You've broken trust.

Okay, maybe it wasn't you personally, but it was someone who came before you. It could have been the last Agile coach or the former chief information officer (CIO) or a chief executive officer (CEO) a few CEOs ago, but you'll still be the one that has to undo the past harm before you can begin anew.

These days, most employees have been through countless false starts at improvement, mostly all at their expense. When you say the name of a popular improvement method—Lean, Agile, and so on—you may hear a noticeable gasp or see people wince or freeze. Clearly, that's a wound.

And let me close the simple solution door. You won't heal the wound with platitudes of "this time it will be different" or worse, ignoring it because "I didn't do it." The bystander defense doesn't work here!

Their reaction, their repulsion at the thought of a change or method isn't resistance; it's damage. They associate that method with personal pain. Your opportunity as the change agent who drives change, not people, is to treat these wounds so they can heal.

Your first step in wound care is to **Honor Their Pain.** When you notice the reaction, comment on the reaction and their pain, and ask if they will share their experiences.

Try saying:

Hi.

I'm here to talk with you today about our new quality initiative.

(Sigh)

(Groan)

(Can you see my eye roll from space?)

I noticed some reactions when I said "quality initiative."

I'm assuming I'm not the first person to talk to you about quality.

If you're willing to share how your last quality initiative experience went, I'd love to listen.

Well...

And then...

That one time...

They said.... but then...

Prepare for the deluge. It may start as a trickle, but the deluge is in there. People like it when someone listens to them, and they appreciate being understood. You will learn a lot about the wounds in just one conversation.

Now pause. Thank them for sharing. Judge whether to move on to the next step now or wait. Rushing on to what comes next may trigger the pain all over again. It will seem counterintuitive. Will reopening the wound help it heal? Yes.

When you're dealing with a physical wound, sometimes you can speed up the healing by opening up the wound through a process call debriding, removing the dead tissue so new tissue can form. Honoring their pain is a lot like debriding a physical wound.

Next, **state your intentions.** You're different, but they don't know that. They assume you are here to Drive People just like all the people before you. Declare and show how different you are.

Try saying:

> What I hear you saying is that in the last quality initiative, the person in my role used
>
> a lot of force and coercion to get you to change.
>
> I call that Driving People.
>
> Sadly, that's how most people think they should create change.
>
> It's likely not comforting to know that they did that because they didn't know any better, but
>
> I can confidently say that's probably why they did what they did to you.
>
> I intend to lead down a different path this time.
>
> *(Allow me to give you funny, skeptical looks.)*

(Does my furrowed brow suggest that I can't tell yet if I can believe you?)

(It should.)

I believe in this change, and I intend to do everything I can to achieve it and clear the obstacles for you so you'll be excited to achieve it with me.

That we have to improve quality isn't up for debate, but how we do it together is what we get to create together.

I intend to Drive Change, not people.

That means I'll choose the change myself and clear the obstacles so you can decide if you want to choose it too.

My focus will be on quality and how we can improve it together, not on a list of orders you have to follow, even if (or especially if) the environment actually doesn't support those changes.

I'm sure you've got questions for me, and I'm happy to answer them now and anytime in the days to come.

(I can feel my face relaxing.)

(I'm not staring off in the distance; I'm thinking of my next question.)

(What about...)

(Last time...)

(But then...)

Don't react to the tone of their questions. Remember, this is the hurt speaking and not a reflection of you and your intentions. I've seen too many good change agents thrown off their intentions in this first meeting, reacting negatively to the negativity they face. Steel yourself to let their hurt out without it hurting you. Compassion is the emotion of the day. Feel it. Live it.

Now, **Walk the Talk 100%.** Yes, 100%, or at least be authentic and vulnerable as you try for perfection.

Why try for perfection? Because they will look for any bit of Driving People from you to prove you do not differ from anyone who has come before you. If you're still new to Driving Change, this will be the hardest step for you because your habits are all around what others should do and how to get the authority to compel them to do it. If you're new to Driving Change, tell them so they can help you not slip back into old habits of Driving People.

Throughout, remember that you didn't cause their wound, but you are now challenged to care for it and heal it if you hope to create your change with them.

Finally, wound care may be the most satisfying of the tactics included in this book because it is the one that produces long-lasting results for those you treat and who heal. Imagine all you can accomplish once people aren't marred by past changes!

And when you return to those methods you've tried and failed at in the past, you can now unlock the improved business performance, job security, and personal pride that come from implementing through Driving Change.

Our only hope, and their only hope, is that those who care enough to take another road and choose to Drive Change reclaim the benefits of Lean, Agile, quality, and more for our organizations and our fellow employees.

Follow the three wound care steps, and then find quick wins you can celebrate together. Each celebration will strengthen the association between you and the change with positive results and emotions. Repeat this regularly to gain even more strength.

• • •

I once ran a global Agile community, a network of people committed to advancing their Agile skills and spreading Agile thinking and methods. Part of my role was to connect with people and encourage them to join our community. Yes, people gasped in pain when I said I wanted to talk to them about Agile. But it was through practicing wound care—honoring their experiences, telling them how I would be different and walking my talk—that I could surface what didn't work with Agile implementations in the past and offer them a new path toward learning and using Agile to speed up their work. This tactic is simultaneously simple and powerful.

WOUND CARE STEPS

1. Honor their pain
2. State your intentions
3. Walk the talk 100%

12
LET THE CONSCRIPTS LEAVE

If we do meet again, we'll smile indeed;
If not, 'tis true this parting was well made.

—William Shakespeare, Julius Caesar

Goal—Get team members to participate

Status Quo Tactic—When they don't participate, chase them and force them back

Change Tactic—Move forward with your advocates, and let the others leave

Why—Because a team of volunteers outperforms a team of conscripts every day

Status Quo Tactic—Our typical change teams are filled with conscripts—people others have forced to join our change. We struggle to get them to come to our mandatory meetings, to take part when they are there, to catch up on progress when they've been absent, or to complete the actions we've agreed to take.

Project managers sink a ton of time into team members' care and feeding—setting, reminding, chasing, and tattling on grown adults. How frustrating!

When people won't participate, beyond pouring time into chasing them and holding their hands through tasks, we have to spend our time trying to get our attention or their boss's attention to make the conscripts participate. We worry that if we tell on them, we will get even less help, but we believe we have no other options when all our chasing, pleading, and more have failed.

We also know that some of these conscripts who rarely show up are the same people who will refuse any decisions that are made without them, so they hold our change hostage to their participation rate.

Have you ever had someone cancel a meeting because one person didn't attend? Have they ever canceled the meeting even after many people had already arrived? Even worse, have you ever been at a meeting where the team spent 10 to 15 minutes at the start of the meeting trying to track down the person who was missing, only to either not find them or find out they aren't coming and didn't tell anyone? After you'd wasted more than 15 minutes, was the meeting canceled?

I've been to that meeting too. It's frustrating!

When you're working with conscripts, the worst behaviors of the worst teammates hold back the success of the advocates, the people who truly want to participate, who attend all the meetings, offer suggestions, and take action. Many team leaders don't allow these advocates to go forward faster out of fear of losing alignment with the conscripts. Some leaders even reverse decisions made without conscripts present, thus further weakening the advocates.

With all these negatives, why do we keep leading teams of conscripts?

Because we don't think we can make progress without them. What if we could?

• • •

Change Tactic—The best tactic would be to Drive Change from the start and form a team of only advocates, thus eliminating the need for this tactic, but we aren't all starting fresh.

Today, if you're leading a team of conscripts, a holdover from your days of Driving People, then this is a perfect quick tactic to get yourself a lot of time back and know where your genuine support lies.

It's a simple tactic—let the conscripts leave.

Your job is to make it as easy as possible for people to show you if they have committed themselves to this change and if they are committed to support their acceleration. If they're not, let them go.

You can quickly sort your advocates from your conscripts by switching your meeting notice from mandatory to optional attendance. By intentionally setting the meeting as optional, you signal that they have the agency to decide to take part or not. In my experience, they will quickly use that agency, and you'll get a clear starting signal of who is on the team and who isn't.

Next, you can reach out to all that declined the optional meeting, one by one, to understand their reasons. Not all who leave were conscripts; some were advocates with conflicts. If they have a meeting conflict, you can either move the meetings or make them part of your team as a relay member (see Tactic 20—Create Your Relay Team). Perhaps they were conscripts who don't care about your change and are grateful to put it behind them. Thank them for their participation, and wish them well.

Don't take a conscript's lack of interest in your change personally or as an indictment of your change. Chances are good that though your change is important, the work they are doing is a higher priority for them, so let them do it.

When you look at your remaining advocates and find you are missing some specific skills or role, the fastest way to fill it is to ask everyone on the team if they know anyone they can ask to join the team. Many people will accept an invitation from a friend or colleague to join a team, especially if the invitation highlights the person's special skills and how the team is excited to learn from and partner with them as an expert.

If you're a rare case where there is only one person who has the skill you need and they aren't available to join you or are refusing to join, that is a great time to partner with a sympathetic leader in the organization to create redundancy in that skill in the organization, whether through an external contract partner, a professional affiliation, or a new hire. No organization should allow itself to be held hostage to the availability or preferences of one person. That's bad for the person and the organization, so you can be grateful this change situation surfaced this organizational risk.

Now let's go back to your team of advocates who want to be with you on this change journey.

You'll find that when you have a team full of people who want to be there, you will get a lot more done a lot faster. You will have to chase people much less.

Free of the conscripts, you will hear from the advocates more, and they will get to make a bigger difference. They will love that. Many times, I've seen these newly energized teams suddenly want to go faster than the project manager. If you're the project manager, that's a fantastic problem to have.

• • •

When Henrietta switched her team from more than 20 conscripts to only four or five advocates, she went from spinning in place, frustratingly trying to meet all their demands, to fast, focused progress. All she had to do was tell the entire team that if they didn't want to be there, they didn't have to be; this is an optional, not mandatory, meeting.

Small-but-mighty is the term for the team that successfully lets the conscripts leave.

13

CHECK FOR CLARITY

Would you tell me, please, which way I ought to go from here?
That depends a good deal on where you want to get to,
said the Cat.
I don't much care where—said Alice.
Then it doesn't matter which way you go,
said the Cat.

—Lewis Carroll, Alice's Adventures in Wonderland

Goal—Reach a common goal together

Status Quo Tactic—Repeat where we said we are going

Change Tactic—Check for clarity to be sure we are
going to the same place

Why—Because if we don't all agree on where we're
going, we'll never get there

Status Quo Tactic—When we worry that our change audience doesn't understand our change, we focus on telling them again and again what we've already told them about our change. We repeat, and we remind. We try to get them to repeat what we've told them.

If they've asked you to repeat the vision statement or the list of values but have never asked what these mean to you, you've seen this status quo. We confuse hearing or remembering with understanding.

Years ago, a judge asked my lawyer husband to meet him at Starbucks after court to discuss a case. My husband nodded and walked away, only later to realize he hadn't asked, "Which Starbucks?" They were in Portland, Oregon, and Portland, like all major cities, has several Starbucks locations near any downtown spot. My husband diligently tried to find out which location by reaching out to the judge's administrative assistant, but she didn't know which one either. My husband never got coffee with the judge. That's a simple story, but it occurs daily in most organizations.

We think we are clear; we rush ahead, we cannot meet, we go back, and we try to start again.

Change Tactic—Never assume you or those around you have clarity. Always check. This is the core assumption under the military tactics of briefing and back briefing to ensure that some heard what we said. We can use a simple version of this tactic in our changes.

Ask 10 people:

When you hear about Change A, what do you say it is about?

Be ready to listen to what aspects of the change story they are pulling out. Be ready to hear some change scars. You may not have known about the scars, or you may have thought they weren't affecting this change. Prepare to be surprised.

Then improve your change statement. Specify and test your Concrete Goal.

<Who> will <experience> <what> <where> <when>.

Ask them:

If I said, <Concrete Goal,> where would you meet me?

Clarify your Concrete Goal until you're confident that if the order went out today—"Everyone meet me at the start of Change A"—you would find each other.

Dilek Ciplak, one of the earlier reviewers of this book, reminded me how we humans would achieve more if we remembered some tactics we don't forget when we work with machines.

In code, we know it isn't enough to send a signal. We confirm it was received and that the proper action was taken.

When we work with people, we assume they will receive and respond, but we don't check. The simplicity of this tactic is to not assume; check.

• • •

There once was an organization behind on its deliverables. Wanting to regain the pace to meet the schedule, the senior leader ordered all the engineers to work 10 hours of mandatory overtime. The senior leader's assumption was that if they worked overtime, they would produce more deliverables.

The engineers begrudgingly worked their overtime, but their output of deliverables didn't go up. The senior leader grew frustrated. He changed his order from 10 hours of mandatory overtime during the week to 10 hours of mandatory overtime each Saturday. At this, the engineers yelled in frustration and again begrudgingly complied. Still, the deliverables rate didn't go up.

A young change agent, puzzled at the situation, suggested that the manager change the order from mandatory overtime to an announcement of the importance of meeting the schedule and asking the engineers to deliver more of the deliverables as soon as possible with the caveat that overtime was available if they needed it.

After the first week, deliverables were up, and overtime was down.

Check for clarity. Is what you're asking for really what you want? And is what they are hearing what you want them to hear?

14

FROM CONSENSUS TO COMMITMENT

Commitment is a function of two things: clarity and buy-in.

—Patrick Lencioni

Goal—Build alignment to build momentum

Status Quo Tactic—Force consensus so you can hold people accountable for momentum

Change Tactic—Build commitment to fuel consensus and momentum

Why—Because momentum earned is momentum preserved

Status Quo Tactic—When you're Driving People, the tactic is to drive for consensus on the team, hoping this agreement will motivate people to take action and commit to the change.

Forced or coerced consensus is superficial and fleeting.

Team members will politely agree or stay quiet in meetings, only to ignore or defy agreement in the following days or weeks. Any purported power in the consensus never materializes.

Pushing for progress from our conscripts, we assume that if we can get them to agree to actions, we have permission to hold them accountable. The conversation goes like this:

> You said you would, so I'm justified in telling on you to your boss when you don't.
>
> *My boss is too busy to worry about you yelling about me.*
>
> *I only said yes to get you to let me leave the meeting.*
>
> Yeah, well... oh.
>
> Yeah, well, please do what you said.
>
> Please.
>
> *Please!*

When our first consensus trap fails, we try to set another one, assuming that if we have the conversation again, this time their commitment will be real. Changes get trapped in this spin of false hope.

True consensus comes after commitment, not before it.

● ● ●

Change Tactic—When you are Driving Change, you are starting from your commitment and gathering others who also want to commit. This commitment fuels people to get to consensus. When I care enough to commit, I care enough to compromise or innovate so we don't have to compromise.

When you are starting with commitment, the risk in consensus is that you achieve it too easily because everyone is excited to say yes and move forward. You can guard against accidental confusion by doing a Simple Consensus Check.

The goal of the Simple Consensus Check is for everyone to share their thoughts. They can elaborate or change after they hear other people's answers. That prevents a false sense of agreement that could form if people share one at a time and soften their actual answers to match the group.

• • •

I can't tell you a specific time where I heard this conversation. In the years of my professional career before I discovered the power of Driving Change, not people, it happened so many times that they all blur together.

Last time we all agreed to Task A, but none of you have done Task A.

So let's discuss again why we must do Task A by next week.

I couldn't because...

I don't understand Task A.

Why next week?

Did you do Task A? No? Well...

Can we move on?

Okay, so we're all agreed that you will do Task A by next week?

Hey, the meeting is not done yet.

You can't leave yet.

Well, okay, I'll see you next week, right?

Right?

Please?

SIMPLE CONSENSUS CHECK

Give each team member a few minutes to write what they think they are being asked to agree to.

Then ask them to rank their commitment to take the action on a scale of 1 to 10 (1 is no commitment, and 10 is intense commitment).

Once everyone has written their statement and scored it, ask them to share it, ideally simultaneously by posting it in a chat box or turning in the paper they wrote on.

Look first at the distribution of commitment scores. That will tell you how hot or cold your team is toward the direction you're headed together.

Then discuss what people thought they were agreeing to. The descriptions will reveal why the scores vary.

A very interesting pattern may be that people scored the action similarly but assumed they were taking two very different actions.

This tactic is quick to implement in any meeting and takes maybe 10 minutes, but it can have a profound effect on the transparency of the agreements and allow for improving the alignment and commitment of the team to their personal role in making it happen.

Technical note: Some people do this through confidence voting, people showing with their hands a score of commitment, from zero (a fist) to five (an open hand with all fingers pointed up). Others use tools for polling the audience in their online meeting platforms. Use the specific process that works best for you in your situation.

FROM HELPLESS TO EMPOWERED

*Being the captain of a nuclear-powered submarine
can be a tremendous rush.
You give orders, people jump, the reactor goes to higher power,
the submarine surges through the water.
You want more, you give more orders,
and you become more controlling.
It has a seductive pull on the leaders, but it is debilitating and
energy sapping for the followers.*

—L. David Marquet, *Turn the Ship Around!*

Goal—Enable people capable of directing and sustaining the change

Status Quo Tactic—Reinforce learned helplessness through Driving People

Change Tactic—Unleash intent through Driving Change

Why—Because they'll never act until we create the space for them to try

Status Quo Tactic—Nuclear-powered submarine captains aren't the only leaders who feel a rush of power that comes from leadership. Many leaders issue orders to change and expect the organization to surge forward under the power of their dictate. Unfortunately for the leaders and their constituents, the actual result is not a surge of power but a puff of defeat.

The half-life of the defeat is long. You wait for orders, resist through passivity, or delay through indifference because you've learned that you don't have to confront your own limitations or risk not succeeding. You can put all the risk for success or failure onto the change leader.

If only they had given us better direction sooner, then we would have succeeded.

At its most extreme, this passivity manifests as a condition of habitually giving up without even trying to succeed. Martin Seligman and colleagues discovered the phenomenon in 1967 and called it **Learned Helplessness.**

According to Seligman and his colleagues, we become infected with learned helplessness "when experience with uncontrollable events leads to the expectation that future events will elude control, disruptions in motivation, emotion, and learning may occur." People suffer a pattern of experiences where they cannot mitigate the pain of change. Faced with this pattern, they fall into learned helplessness because, as Seligman says in *Learned Optimism:*

When we overestimate our helplessness,
other forces will take control.

Seligman and team found that rats or dogs that were repeatedly placed in conditions where they received a shock and could not escape it or turn it off learned to lie down and accept the pain. People experiencing the pain of repeated imposed changes beyond their influence also quickly learn it is hopeless to try.

Realizing this hopelessness and hoping to correct it, some leaders try to remove the pain and assume that people will spring back to action. Sadly, removing whatever was making the conditions inescapable (the shock for the rat or dog) or the policies or leaders doesn't cure the learned helplessness. Only repeated experiences with agency heal the helplessness. Agency, as Seligman defines it, is:

One's belief that they can change the world for the better.

Research suggests it can take between 30 and 50 experiences with agency before a person cures their helplessness.

A person suffering from learned helplessness assumes that their actions cannot bring about success, so it is better to not try but to freeze in place and wait for the pain to pass. Learned helplessness is rampant in most organizations, and managers are often ignorant of the condition or the cure.

I once coached a manager suffering with the consequences of learned helplessness. He had recently implemented a policy that specified the steps through which a technician could decide to proceed. The problem was that this policy came after a year when the technicians were repeatedly told they didn't understand the work well enough to decide anything.

When the managers finally gave the technicians some control over their work, the technicians either blindly complied with the policy or froze. The policy told the technician what to do if a reading was above a set point and what to do if a number was below a set point, but it didn't say what to do if the reading was exactly at the set point. It said, "Use your discretion." It shocked the manager that the technicians refused to use their discretion. They insisted that the policy tell them what to do.

Ultimately, the manager changed the policy to state what to do when the reading was exactly the right number. That only mitigated the worst consequences of the learned helplessness but didn't cure it. To cure it would require them to change tactics.

• • •

Change Tactic—When we Drive Change, we role model trying new things ourselves, learning, adapting, and trying again. When we invite others to learn with us and make it safe for them to do so, we help them regain their active engagement in the change, help them build a sense of personal accountability for the change, and leave them stronger and more proactive for the next change.

Anyone can create space for others to regain their agency and cure their learned helplessness. What you can do today is to stop telling others what to do. Refuse to order others. Instead, ask them:

What do you think we should do?

What can I do to help you do that?

Follow that up with more curiosity and support.

Why do you think that will work?

What might go wrong?

How would we monitor for or prevent that risk?

Then help them move forward. If they are trapped in learned helplessness, you'll have to help them those 30 to 50 times before they self-initiate again. You can speed yourself through those 30+ repetitions by creating opportunities for them to decide on their own every day or several times a day. Don't wait for bi-weekly team meetings and expect to cure the learned helplessness quickly.

For more information on this tactic, read L. David Marquet's *Turn the Ship Around!* in which he explains his concept of intent-based leadership and tells many powerful sea stories we can learn from.

Marquet transformed from a leader with all the answers to a leader who empowered everyone on the nuclear-powered submarine to lead. In his time in command of USS *Santa Fe* (SSN-763), he learned the power of intent-based leadership, and his crew learned how to create individual and group improvement and went on to successful careers and command tours of their own.

The key is first shifting to the philosophy of Driving Change and then leveraging all the opportunities to live the change and clear the obstacles for others to choose it too. You'll find that continual cultivation of agency inoculates you and your organization from the ill of learned helplessness.

• • •

In 2016, Captain Marquet agreed to write the Foreword to *Everyone Is a Change Agent*. In part, he wrote:

> Change is a ubiquitous aspect of life and leading change is an essential part of leadership. Every leader is a change agent. At the end of the day, the only person we can control is our self. Attempts to control others always result in manipulation, bad feelings and a sense of being let down.

To that I'll add, "and create learned helplessness." Captain Marquet and I commit to creating empowerment, not helplessness. Join us.

FROM HELPLESS TO EMPOWERED WORKSHEET

Your goal: Create 30 to 50 experiences with agency for your target audience.

Agency: One's belief that they can change the world for the better.

You get a gold star for any action you can take to switch from ordering to agency, but it still only counts as one experience.

You can use this template to plan and track your experiences.

Go! Go as fast as you can.

Watch for unprompted agency. That's when you'll know you're close to the cure. Don't let up!

#	Experience / Action
1	
2	
3	
4	
5	
6	
7	
8	
9	
10	
11	
12	
13	
14	
15	
16	
17	
18	
19	
20	
21	
22	

#	Experience / Action
23	
24	
25	
26	
27	
28	
29	
30	
31	
32	
33	
34	
35	
36	
37	
38	
39	
40	
41	
42	
43	
44	

#	Experience / Action
45	
46	
47	
48	
49	
50	

16
FIND YOUR HIDDEN
CHANGE AGENTS

There are no good people waiting to be hired.
All of the good people already have jobs.

—Admiral H. G. Rickover

Goal—Fill your organization with highly capable
change agents

Status Quo Tactic—Hire change agents from outside
the organization

Change Tactic—Find your hidden change agents

Why—Your change agents aren't missing; they're
dormant and ready to awaken

Status Quo Tactic—We assume that if we have good change agents inside our organizations, they have already created our changes. Since they haven't, we assume we need to find the *right people* outside our organization. Who are the **right people**? They are people who will respond correctly when we drive them to change, of course.

I've watched change efforts stall for six months or more while the team frantically tried to recruit, interview, select, and onboard these *right people*. Then once they were onboard, there was always a delay as they learned their role and the organization.

If you follow this path, a year after the hiring conversation, you may have someone in place. What you quickly find after that is the timing of the change has already passed or worse. You still need the change, but this new person still isn't enough to force the change. Your hunt for resumes for the next *right person*.

We may wonder if the people we have could learn the competencies for the change we want, but we don't take action on this because the people seem too helpless to be good change agents. They resist the changes we force upon them. They ignore our demands for more and more compliance with our latest change of the moment. They seem beyond redemption.

What was the last change each of them got excited about?

If we asked that question, we would quickly have a list of changes the organization has attempted. Everyone has some answer to that question. I've never met a person who had no answer to this question. So everyone was the *right person* for a certain change.

Why do most people often seem so passive and beyond redemption?

Martin Seligman calls their condition Learned Helplessness. We covered learned helplessness in Tactic 15—From Helpless to Empowered.

The sad facts are that first we made them powerless by driving them to change, and then we tried to replace them.

We should listen to the words of a noted leader of transformative change, Delancy founder Mimi Silbert, when she says, "I can't say strongly enough how much powerlessness corrupts" (quoted in *Change or Die*).

We have to solve our powerless problem, or any hiring will only produce the conditions we have already.

• • •

Change Tactic—Learned helplessness is just as it says—learned. It's not inherent in who people are, so that means we don't have to replace them. We can and should help them unlearn their helplessness or, as Seligman suggests, help them learn optimism.

The best way I've found to teach people optimism is to Drive Change and also help them to Drive Change—change in their lives, their work, and their communities. If you do, you'll focus on the good (what can go right), and you'll unlock the best in your people and the world.

You can't just Drive Change once and hope they've got it. You actually have to stick with it long after you think:

They should have learned something by now.

What you're targeting is the connection the people make between their behavior and the outcome they get.

What learned helplessness taught them is this:

No matter what I do, nothing changes.

You're working to replace that with the Change Agent's Motto:

I will do what I can, with what I have, where I am.

And you're helping them notice the success of their actions.

Because you did A with B, we now have C and can do D.

Thank you!

What do you think we should do next together?

Seligman and team learned "that most voluntary behavior is motivated by what you expect the behavior will cause."

Help your employees believe that good things for them and for your organization can result from their voluntary behaviors, and you'll get more and more positive voluntary behaviors that drive your changes forward.

• • •

If I've heard it once, I've heard it a thousand times. We don't have the *right people* on this change. After the thousandth time, my reply has gotten snippy:

You do not know who the right people are.

I then proceed quickly to build a team with change agents the leaders never knew they had.

Decades into Driving Change, I count multitudes of change agents as dear friends, most of whom their leaders didn't consider to be the *right people* until the change agents broke free from learned helplessness perpetuated by others who were Driving People. These *right people* drove change and proved how amazing they were.

If you don't think you have the *right people*, you are probably Driving People. Stop that! Drive Change, and the *right people* will quickly reveal themselves.

One winter long ago, I honored these *right people* who had revealed themselves. Using dollar-store jingle bell garland, small pieces of ribbon, a safety pin, and a bit of hot glue, I built change agent medals. I gave them to all the change agents I knew. I gave out more than 200 medals. The special bonus of these medals was that any change agent wearing the medal announced their presence as they walked down the hall or into the room with a gentle, sweet jingle, jingle ring.

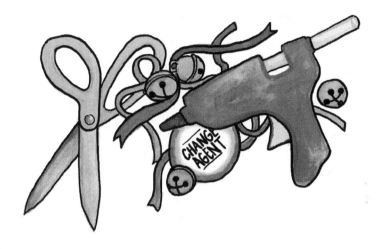

HIDDEN CHANGE AGENT FINDER

Here are two methods you can use to find the hidden change agents within your organization.

Method 1: Ask for volunteers; then invest in them.

This method replaces selecting (aka conscripting) team members.

Have criteria for who you'll select from the volunteers. You don't have to allow everyone who volunteers to join you. But be wary of your criteria. While you may keep out the riffraff, you will also potentially leave out skilled change agents.

Watch for those you don't select who fight to join anyway. They are your amazing, untapped change agents. The best change agents choose themselves and refuse to be left on the sidelines.

With all volunteers, start by introducing them to Driving Change. Their internal spark of energy got them there. Help them use their spark to spark others.

Method 2: Watch for sparklers; then make them safe.

In Tactic 15—From Helpless to Empowered, the worksheet leads you through planning and executing a series of experiences to reduce learned helplessness and increase agency. To watch for sparklers is to observe who responds most positively and most strongly to your experiences with agency.

If someone joins your next meeting to offer suggestions and get involved, they are your hidden change agents.

If you notice something great going on in your organization that you didn't order people to do, ask around to learn who took that action; that's a hidden change agent.

If you encounter a wonderful new service or feature in your organization, investigate who was behind it. They are your hidden change agents.

And finally, ask around for names of people who have refused to let certain changes die or who advocated for the changes before you even suggested them. They are your hidden change agents.

Once you find the sparklers, introduce them to Driving Change. Filled with raw talent, these change agents have the internal motivation to go far. Introducing them to Driving Change will help them go farther faster.

STUDY THE HOMETOWN PROPHETS

*Prophets are honored everywhere except
in their own hometowns and in their own households.*

—Matthew 13:57, Common English Bible

Goal—Find the best change advocates as soon as possible

Status Quo Tactic—We assume no one is doing the change until we tell them to do it

Change Tactic—There are advocates for this change; I just have to find them

Why—Because changes aren't as new as we think they are

Status Quo Tactic—Many change teams assume that until they began, no one was trying to change. They give an order and watch for who jumps, assuming that these people will be the best advocates. This is Driving People thinking—assuming that until you've given the order, no one can advocate change.

Before the quality effort, the team assumes no one cares about quality or we wouldn't need this change. Before the Agile implementation, there must be no one doing Agile (even though Agile started at the grassroots in nearly every company where it has taken hold and succeeded). Before diversity goals, there must have been nobody who was successfully recruiting and retaining diverse talent. These are all flavors of the flawed assumption that unless everyone is doing it, no one is doing it.

None of these changes are new, even if they are new to the leaders attempting to force the change on the organization. Consultants hired from the outside to force a change know this truth. The consultants seek the local change agents who leaders have previously repeatedly ignored, interview them, and report their interview results as findings. The leader beams with pride at their smarts to hire the consultant to lead them into the future. The local change agents are more frustrated than they were before.

• • •

Change Tactic—The thing about biblical truths is that they show us how long humanity has suffered from the same misconceptions. The biblical statement that no one is a prophet in their hometown proves true in many change situations. We can flip it on its head too. Every hometown likely has a prophet it has overlooked until now.

These hometown prophets are obviously a treasure trove of support for our change, but even more so they are a fount of information of what didn't work before and why. If it had all been successful when they were trying, there would be more of them, and they wouldn't need the change this time.

When I've met these hometown prophets and they've shared their stories, the classic reason for their lack of success is that they were Driving People, not Driving Change. Without the organizational authority or the numbers initially to get the force change to stick, they could never break out of their singular or small group support for the change.

You now can show them Driving Change, help them continue to choose the change for themselves, and clear the obstacles for them to partner with you to create the change they have been seeking all along.

• • •

The plight of hometown prophets absent this tactic is one of my driving forces behind writing this book. I've seen too many people retire or quit in frustration before the leadership caught up to their visions or before the mixture of leadership and tactics was right to create their change.

Once after an organization had purged an extensive list of its best Agile advocates through a major layoff, a leader called me to ask if I knew any Agile coaches. My terse reply was:

Why are you asking?

I wasn't as polite as I usually am. When I explained that the list of names I would have given him was several times longer than only a month before, I shocked him. He never knew all the value those people could have brought, and by the time he learned it, it was too late.

TIPS TO FIND AND SUPPORT THE HOMETOWN PROPHETS

- **Ask around.**
  Have you ever heard of <fill in the change> (i.e., Agile, lean, quality, etc.)? If so, who did you hear it from?
  If someone says no, ask someone else. Don't stop until you've asked at least 20 people.
- **Ask several times.**
  Are you sure you've never heard of anyone around here advocating for <fill in the change>?
  Depending on how wounded these people have been from

their past attempts, they might not want to reveal themselves or their friends to you, even (or especially) if they still care about the change.

- **Learn about last time.**
  How did it go?
  By listening to them with an open heart, you will learn more about the organization you are serving and about the prophet and get to learn from what was potentially a painful experience. You can mitigate future pain by honoring the mistakes of the past.

- **Teach them about Driving Change.**
  You obviously care about the change. Let me help you get others to join you in making it happen.
  Chances are good that they had the first part of Driving Change (choosing the change for themselves) but not the second (clearing the obstacles for others to choose it too). If they had a different way of change role modeled to them before when they first tried to create the change, they would have had better results. You can help them see the problem wasn't the change or them; it was the tactic they used to create the change.

- **Help them join you.**
  How would you like to be involved? What can I do to make that happen?
  They will each have their own ideal way to be involved. If they want to be included in the change but need your support for their role, scope, and involvement with leadership, then partner with them and work toward making time and space for this to happen. To reattempt something that has failed is courageous, it is worth negotiating with leadership to have that person on the team.

- **Develop the change together.**
  How might we...
  They may have tons of learning experience in the organization, so you can leverage the power of their collective intelligence.

- **Lead them across the finish line.**
  Let's go!
  Help them share and spread the change vision and speed up the change together.

18
BUILD A TEAM FULL OF SUPERHEROES

Wear your cape like you earned it, because you did.

—April K. Mills

Goal—Field an amazing change team

Status Quo Tactic—Conscript the *best people* over and over again

Change Tactic—Help your amazing superheroes discover their superpowers

Why—Because people just need a bit of encouragement to amaze you and them

Status Quo Tactic—We start our change efforts by demanding that leaders assign the *best people* to our team. We define *best people* as those people possessing the perfect mix of authority (or access to it) and knowledge of the change topic.

To get these *best people* on the team, they will certainly have to be conscripted—their boss assigns them to the team at your request. These *best people* are very busy because their mix of experience and authority has them in high demand. You'll struggle to find a spot on their calendars, they won't attend your team meeting regularly, and they'll often refuse to accept an action even if you've tried to craft it to get the best out of their expertise. Overly conscripted on multiple teams, on top of their day jobs, the *best people* hesitate to offer to complete tasks and may even resist any actions you try to give them.

Some teams go through several waves of the *best people* before they find a quorum of people willing to work on the change. Sometimes leaders cancel the change before the team actually figures out who the *best people* would have been.

Meanwhile, there's that pesky person who kept trying to join your team, your meetings, your events. They lack the seniority, authority, or experience to be a *best person* for the change. Chances are good that you placated them by suggesting that at some unspecified *later* they might get involved. Without the other *best people*, that *later* never came.

• • •

Change Tactic—The truly **best people** are the people who are (1) excited about your change and (2) willing to Drive Change, not people. You can cultivate authority and access experience, but you can't succeed without passion to overcome the obstacles you'll face and a commitment to finding the way to do it together with your team and your organization.

Freed from the assumption that they should wait to be asked, the most outstanding change agents emerge from organizations if only we will look for them. Rather than searching for a needle in the haystack, you can create a magnet that attracts those needles to you by saying:

Who wants to drive this change with me?

Then, when a change agent lives the Change Agent's Motto (I will do what I can, with what I have, where I am), they find their superpower naturally.

Maybe it is a flair for winning advocates or finding experts or painting a picture of what can be once you're past the next enormous obstacle. The options are endless. Behind each of these superpowers is their resourcefulness to do what it takes to make this change happen.

You can help them find their superpower by asking:

What will you do with what you have, where you are, to advance this change?

Then help them do what they suggest, and you'll watch their superpower emerge.

• • •

Once upon a time there was a team trying to expand the ways employees learned about the latest organizational news. Digital displays in hallways and elevator lobbies were becoming the hottest trend in employee communications. After a team meeting where someone suggested we consider electronic displays as one of our initiatives, a young man named Phill revealed his superpower.

Entirely on his own initiative, Phill spent days in the community looking for all the ways businesses and organizations were sharing messages electronically. The next week, he surprised the team with a presentation on multiple options that were already present in our organization and community, so we could consider our next steps from a list of practical options, not just concepts. Phill's superpower was in seeing the options all around him that other people missed. He used this superpower on countless teams in the years that followed, and he remains a superhero that I'll always be proud to have served alongside.

Bonus: You can watch Phill present some of his Guiding Coalition work in this video: https://tinyurl.com/2010P-C-Part3

BUILD A TEAM FULL OF SUPERHEROES CHECKLIST

Follow these steps to remind you of the simple steps to form a team of superheroes.

Add to this checklist as you learn your way forward.

Checklist Item	Done?
Craft your three-minute story about your change to share and find your change agent superheroes.	
Pick three events to tell your change story so you can find and enroll the change agent superheroes. 1. 2. 3.	
Introduce them to Driving Change, not people, and confirm that they will Drive Change, not people, with you. Note: Continually monitor this if it is their first try at Driving Change. Old habits of Driving People are hard to break. You can tell if they've slipped back if they tell others what to do instead of acting themselves and helping others join them.	
Define their superpowers: • They can declare their superpower, or • You can help them reveal their superpower. Ask: *What do you think your superpower is, and how do you want to offer it?* • If they don't know, you could suggest something if you know them. • They can ask five people who know them well what those people would say their superpower is.	
Help them practice their superpower, and review how their practice went: • If good, do it again. • If not, adjust and try something else.	
Share what superpowers your team most needs, and ask them if they would like to build that superpower (i.e., project planning, stakeholder management, contact with advocates).	

19

SHINE A LIGHT ON THE INVISIBLE PEOPLE

Example is not the main thing.
It is the only thing.

—Albert Schweitzer

Goal—Find role models for the change

Status Quo Tactic—Try to conscript the senior leaders to be role models

Change Tactic—Shine a light on the invisible people who are already role models

Why—Current, consistent role models immediately strengthen your change

Status Quo Tactic—When we are Driving People, we are constantly seeking the highest potential leader to be the figurehead of our change. That propels us to want the highest senior leader and their surrounding leaders to be seen as the primary role models for our change.

Of course, we want to trade on that senior leader's name.

Bob, the CEO, says...

We also want Bob to live the change for everyone to see so people will think:

Well, since Bob is doing it, I guess I have to do it.

Typically, most leaders are barely willing to lend their names to change and rarely if ever role model the changes they drive onto the people in their organizations.

Sure, you can get them to recite certain phrases in corporate communications.

Quality is job one!

We must all focus on our customers.

And on and on.

But few people ever see the day-to-day activities of these senior leaders. Sadly, when they get a glimpse, it is easier to see how they aren't living up to their words than how they are.

If you try this status quo tactic and succeed, the best you will get is a big-but-paper-thin role model. The worst you will get is a big hypocrite.

• • •

Change Tactic—In every organization, there are people who were doing your change or advocating the change before you started. These are your best role models. They are typically invisible in the organization. No one sees them, and no one cares.

You have the power to shine a light on them and make them visible. They are easy to find. All you have to do is ask.

Who do you know who is doing Change A?

Do you know anyone talking about Change B?

Who would you say is the best role model for Change C?

Ask 50 people these questions, and you'll find at least one. Ask 100 people, and you'll find at least two. And that's all you need. The one or two proves that it is possible to do your change or want your change in this organization.

Talk to them. Have them share their story. Learn what challenges they have faced and overcome. Support them.

Chances are good that these are the role models who have toiled for years invisibly. When senior leaders in the past have advocated for change through words, not deeds, these role models became hurt and frustrated. You're able by honoring them and their role modeling to bring them the recognition they have been too long denied.

There are several extra benefits of this approach:

1. It is faster to find these hidden gems than it is to get the attention of a senior leader. You could ask 50 people via an e-mail right now. Just put this book down and ask them.
2. The people you find are typically in the organization and not at the top of the organization, which makes them much more relatable and approachable for your target change audience. A director who can look to another director who has solved a work flow issue is going to gain a lot more insights than a senior leader who tries to make work flow faster.
3. The role models you find will usually be grateful for the attention to something they've been passionate about for a long time. Typically humble, they will probably ask you to put the attention on the results or their teams versus them, but don't let them step all the way out of the light. The organization is better for their example; help them let their light shine.

4. The role models will be excited to show you how they get their work done, and they will be a key resource of ways to do even better.

5. If the same role models pop up again and again, they are showing you a special power they have to see what the organization needs before the organization knows it. Consider these people for positions of great responsibility and promotion. They have something special you'll want to leverage more and more.

• • •

Many organizations today are working to improve their diversity and inclusion. They have launched major programs to recruit, hire, and retain diverse talent. Some have incentives for their leaders to achieve diversity and inclusion goals. I've seen many senior leaders named as the official champion of the effort and recite the company taglines from keynote stages, but they are not actual role models for the change. Twice, I saw something different.

At an industry conference, before a senior leader took the stage to discuss his company's diversity goals, his chief of staff took the stage to introduce him. She let the audience know we were about to hear from someone who didn't just say the right words; he was a proper role model. She told a story of a meeting where she was being talked over by other leaders. Her boss stopped the meeting and said something to this effect:

We won't talk over our colleagues like that.

I want to hear what she has to say.

Please continue...

The second example was my first manager at Intel Corporation, Ray Arell. Long before the industry focus on diversity, Ray had filled his team with the strongest leaders he could find, which included many outstanding women. He didn't wait to be encouraged to find and support the best talent; he lived it spontaneously. We need to shine the light on more leaders like Ray.

20
CREATE YOUR RELAY TEAM

You can't do epic all by yourself:
you get 12 people together, anything is possible.
Strange and wonderful things happen
when you work together as a team.

—Hood to Coast (Jim Ekberg, Team Dead Jocks in a Box)

Goal—Make the most progress in the least amount of time

Status Quo Tactic—Expect either a project manager or a large team to cover every mile

Change Tactic—Create your relay team

Why—Because we make more progress if we each complete our leg of the change

Status Quo Tactic—Most change initiatives have one of these two common structures.

First, there is the solo project manager structure. In this structure, you select a project manager who is expected through pure influence to gather from the organization the resources necessary to achieve the project. This project manager has no direct reports, and everyone who is considered "on the project" is really just those willing to respond to the project manager's meeting requests.

This structure makes progress through meetings. When they aren't meeting or can't meet because of conflicting schedules, the project stops. Most project managers spend their time securing the agreement of people to attend the meeting and complete their assigned actions.

A noticeable factor of this structure is that most of the people who attend the meetings aren't the people who have to take action to make the project successful; instead, they are representatives of the groups of affected audiences. For example, a director attends on behalf of their larger organization (their peers and their direct reports) and then must rally their employees, peers, and employees to comply with the project.

Second, there is the large conscript team structure. The members are there by force, and this team makes progress only when they can agree on what they will do simultaneously. They meet a lot and agree on some actions, but action is slow because it is difficult to get a large team of conscripts to both agree and act simultaneously.

After months on a team like this, the lack of progress burns out and frustrates the conscripts. Their bosses added this conscripted work on top of their other work, so living with the overload and competing priorities has exhausted them.

After completing a few simple actions, these teams usually disappear as the senior leadership's attention wanes. (Note: Short-tenured senior leaders speed up this process. See Tactic 34—Calibrate the Change to the Half-Lives).

• • •

Change Tactic—Get the most out of your team with the least effort required from each team member. Build a relay team. We model the relay team on one of the best examples of teamwork in the world—Hood to Coast.

Hood to Coast is a team relay race that challenges teams of two to 12 team members to partner and run from Mount Hood (east of Portland, Oregon) to Seaside, Oregon, over a coastal mountain range a distance of more than 200 miles.

Since Bob Foote founded Hood to Coast in 1982, many teams have completed the 200-mile course, and now each year (except 2020) the relay welcomes more than 1,000 teams to compete. Some teams are comprised of elite athletes, some are high school track teams, some are middle-aged joggers looking for an excuse to spend a fun weekend with their friends, and some are ladies over 60 years old who commit to showing themselves and their grandchildren that "Grandma's still got it."

What these teams accomplish together is something that almost no one in the world could do alone. The team members share 36 relay legs (three per teammate) to cover the 200 miles in less than 40 hours. (The record is an elite team that completed the course in less than 16 hours—a pace of under 5 minutes per mile.) Only the world's hyper-elite distance athletes would even attempt that solo. But when you allow regular people to form a team of people who commit to covering the distance together, then they deliver amazing results over 1,000 times in less than two days.

When you leverage this Hood to Coast relay concept to speed up your change, you gather a team of people who want to achieve the change but know they can't do it all themselves. Unlike the team mentioned in the status quo, this relay team doesn't expect everyone to do everything at the same time. Instead, you're looking for what the strengths are of each person or what their conflicts and limitations are, and you're dividing the work to get to the outcome across the group so each of your portions is small but included together produces amazing results.

• • •

A perfect example of a relay team is the Bremerton Beyond Accessible Play team that spent three-and-a-half years launching, fundraising, designing, and building a beyond accessible playground at Evergreen Rotary Park in Bremerton, Washington.

Many of the team members provided consistent support throughout the project, but several were key relay team members we called on and relied on when their talents were most needed.

One team member's relay team experience is important to highlight. Everyone throughout Bremerton knows Mick Hersey as the go-to guy for volunteer outdoor projects. He restores tombstones in historical grave-yards, tends to the graves of veterans, fixes up local monuments, and loves to get involved with special projects like the Beyond Accessible play-ground. Mick wasn't part of the Bremerton Beyond Accessible Play team for all three-and-a-half years. Mick got involved shortly before the build phase of the project. That was the phase where his special skills of finding, coordinating, and leveraging volunteers, especially local sailors, shined.

We would have welcomed Mick any time during the three-and-a-half-year project, but if he had joined us then, he would have been waiting for his time to shine. In the three years we were planning the project, Mick was actively leading many other community projects that were a better use of his talents at those times. It would have been a loss to the community if I had demanded that Mick get involved with our project when we were in our early phases. I would never have wanted to tie up his time waiting for our buildout when he could be doing so much good for so many other people while we got our project to the build phase.

This is the compounding power of a relay team. You get the benefit of their talents at the right time, and so many other teams get the benefit of their talents at their right times. There are too few Mick Herseys in this world. We can do our part to help them have their biggest impact and truly shine!

I've posted an example of the Relay Team Coordination Worksheet for

Bremerton Beyond Accessible Play at https://engine-for-change.com/weblog/relay-team-coordination-worksheet/

RELAY TEAM COORDINATION WORKSHEET

What's your Concrete Goal? That's your finish line.

\<Who\> will \<experience\> \<what\> \<where\> \<when\>.

Who wants to get to run legs of the race to get us to our Concrete Goal?

Name	Talent	Leg(s) of the Race

Describe the handoffs from leg to leg

1 _____

2 _____

3 _____

4 _____

5 _____

6 _____

7 _____

8 _____

Extra suggestion: If you'd love a visual to go with these lists, my friend and colleague Autumn Witherspoon, a phenomenal program and project manager, suggests using the legs as swim lanes and the handoffs as key milestones to build a Relay Team Project Plan. If you try this visualization, remember to preserve the relay benefits and make sure your project plan doesn't expect everyone to be active simultaneously.

21
SAY THEIR NAMES

In the future, everyone will be world famous for 15 minutes.

—Andy Warhol

Goal—Gain the most attention and buy-in for your change

Status Quo Tactic—Constantly bombard people with communications about your change

Change Tactic—Include their names in as many of your communications as possible

Why—Because people remember when others mention them or those they know

Status Quo Tactic—Change managers know the importance of communication to speed up a change. They invest much time and attention in the communication plan. That's good. What's bad is that they leave out names except the name of the senior leader who is Driving People to change.

If you have a change in process right now, review your last few communications and see how many names per communication you used. Go ahead, put this book down and count. I'll wait.

How many names did you find?

More than three per communication? You can probably skip the rest of this section and go on to the change tactic below because you've got great potential to be even better.

Between one and two? That's typical. Most communications only include the name of the person sending it and maybe one other person if the writer has to invoke a higher authority—the VP mentioning that the CEO is behind the change. These communications are for awareness building about who is driving you to change and what will happen if you don't comply. Many times, the leaders invoked are people the employees will never meet personally. This facet of the change is more challenging in large and distributed organizations, especially in situations where many employees are working remotely and will never come face-to-face with many of the leaders named. Maybe in the past, an employee could see a senior leader in person at an all-company meeting or forum and perhaps asked them a question or said hello in the hallway. Now these leaders are as distant as Hollywood celebrities, people we only see on screens and who do not know who we are.

Zero? That's the peak status quo score. How do you score a zero? You've gone to the peak of Driving People, assuming that it isn't even necessary to have a person forcing them. The so-called "faceless account" should be enough to compel them. "IT Communications" declares you must. "Corporate Strategy" expects your alignment. Fill in the quotes with your favorite account you delete as soon as you see it in the "from" column in your inbox. They might as well have not sent these messages.

• • •

Change Tactic—You're right that to get buy-in for your change, people must first know about your change. This insight is why Prosci's ADKAR model starts with awareness. But how you get that awareness needs a major upgrade. The old status quo tactics of bombarding with big messages sent by senior leaders aren't working anymore (if they ever did).

With so many people working from home, multi-tasking while listening to online leadership message forums, and ignoring as many e-mails as possible just to stay sane, you're going to struggle to get attention through traditional communications unless you try this new tactic.

Names. Names. Names. Give them names. Celebrate the names. Share the names. Celebrate the names. (Yes, I said celebrate twice.)

Names are powerful. They draw us in. They draw us together. They show us who will be with us if we join.

We can replace the messages sent from the senior leader or "faceless account" with a message from an actual person I have (or can learn to have) a genuine relationship with. I'm not likely to take action because IT Communications told me to. However, if Gail from IT Communications reaches out to invite me to join her in the latest IT effort, I may read the message and take action. I'm even more likely to act as if I've connected with Gail before and had a wonderful experience.

This leads to the next point: play the long game. Name recognition comes from experience with someone. I need to have stories I share with that person so I know who they are and have some confidence that they know who I am. So don't just include names; tell stories about them. I'm much more likely to read a message that includes the names of everyone on a team and tells me what they did to move the change forward. Even if I don't know any of the people, I'm going to study the message to see if I know someone. And if I find a name of someone I know, I'm more likely to talk about the message again when I see that person next. Now you've created a message half-life of days or weeks instead of milliseconds. That's powerful.

When you're telling stories about teams, don't forget to include the managers' names too. "Managers don't need the praise or attention," you say, but they are people, and they like to see their names too. They have peers and friends who will enjoy seeing their names. Remember, the more names that are included, the more likely someone in your audience knows them and reaches out, or at least reads more closely to see what their friend or colleague is being celebrated for.

We humanize a change when we fill it with names. The change doesn't float above the people ready to strike. Instead, a change filled with people is something that is alive, moving in people's hearts and lives with vibrancy.

Track your names and communication metric. If you're looking for traction in your change, keep driving that metric up. Gather the stories. Celebrate the people. Expand who you mention. You'll see your change grow.

22
PILE UP THE
PARTNERSHIPS

You can call up almost anyone whose help you need,
say you have heard great things about their capabilities,
and ask if you can buy them lunch and pick their brain.
Few people can resist so easy and flattering a request for help.
Having given you advice, they become allies.

—*Gifford Pinchot III, Intrapraneuring*

> Goal—Create a large group of advocates for the change
>
> Status Quo Tactic—Grow the change team to lock people into supporting the change
>
> Change Tactic—Pile up the partnerships with your small team of change agents
>
> Why—Because people who help you once become advocates forever

Status Quo Tactic—We assume that if we compel people, conscript them onto our team, and make them help us plan the change, they will advocate for the change. That rarely works. Instead, it just makes our teams so big that it leads to other problems.

Large teams are also difficult to manage. Timing of meetings is a challenge as the number grows, and keeping a large group aligned involves more communication and status meetings, both of which drain time from people who resented a small investment of time in this forced change, let alone larger time sinks.

It is hard to keep a large team moving forward during planning, and the difficulty increases when you move to implementation. We've added the people, assuming that "many hands make light work," when the work finally needs to be done. What we actually find is that each hand needs to be held, and there are too few truly engaged to do all the holding. That causes the change team, when it should do its most outreach, to be mostly inwardly focused with the change manager spending most of their time reminding, supporting, and cajoling the team members to do what the project plan says they should do.

• • •

Change Tactic—A small team of change agents committed to Driving Change together will outperform a team of conscripts 10 times their size every time.

To grow their influence, the team doesn't need to grow. What they need to focus on is whose help they need the most and how to get that help with the least time investment from the helper. That looks like this: invite them to one meeting to teach you about their area and how you can be most effective. That is in sharp contrast to the status quo tactic—send them a mandatory meeting notice for repeated meetings where they need to be present in case you need them and so they can hear all the actions you will task them with enforcing in their area.

People like to be complimented on what they know. When you invite them to share what they know so you can learn and improve, they will jump at the chance. Set a special time that is convenient for them versus just inviting them to your regular meetings, and they will have a hard time turning you down.

Follow up with them on how you incorporated what they taught you into your change plan, and they will be an advocate for your change. People like to help their advice succeed. And they will do it thinking they are doing you a favor and will feel good about it too. So you'll get the support you need, and they'll feel good doing it. That's hard to beat.

• • •

When we started Bremerton Beyond Accessible Play, one of our first tasks was to present our project goals to the city parks board. I knew many of the board members, but some were unfamiliar faces. We went to the meetings eager to share our project and what we wanted to do for them and hopefully with them. We were Driving Change, so we didn't demand that anyone join us. We only asked that if they had talents they wanted to share, we would love their partnership. That one meeting opened up two powerful partnerships.

Our project goals moved John Larson, a city parks board member. He'd never noticed the barriers to play that he said had been hiding in plain sight. Once we showed him those barriers, he went out the next day to visit the potential playground site and saw the barriers to play for himself. Then he drove 45 minutes to the closest accessible playground to see what a playground with accessible features looked like. He was convinced. He joined our team the following week and was by our side for nearly the whole three-and-a-half-year project.

Sunny Wheeler, another city parks board member, had been an acquaintance of mine for years before the playground project. The project moved her too. Sunny regularly joined our team meetings and helped us move the project along. A most memorable moment of her partnership transforming the project was when she successfully advocated for the Bennett Memorial Scholarship Fund to provide Bremerton Beyond Accessible Play a surprise $30,000 grant, which allowed us to buy key equipment for the playground. On a cold, rainy December night in the city council's regular meeting, Sunny surprised us and the entire audience with the grant.

You can watch the moment and watch me hug Sunny Wheeler to get the full feeling of the power of piling up partnerships. http://tinyurl.com/ TheLast30K.

23

BUILD A TOWER OF SUPPORT

*What's the difference between a Parisian street mime
and an employee going through an organizational change?
The mime knows he's in an invisible box.*

—*April K. Mills*

Goal—Get the best out of our people as soon as
possible

Status Quo Tactic—Create boxes of limitations that the
employees must comply with

Change Tactic—Build a tower of support to help people
reach toward your change

Why—Because people thrive more with support than
limitations

Status Quo Tactic—When we strive to implement a change across a group of people, we think the best way to make the change happen is to be very specific about what employees must and must not do. We also set timelines for how soon people can act and deadlines by when they must act. Though it may not be our intention, the result of the combination of these tendencies is the construction of a small box around each employee, limiting their ability to engage in the change beyond following instructions.

These habits produce several undesirable effects.

1. We stop anyone who knows how to do more to support the change from acting independently.
2. All those who are disinterested in the change know they can wait for the second or third reminder (if that ever happens) to encourage (force) them to complete the change. Experience has taught them that if you delay your action in most changes, the change will fail before you have to take any action.
3. We ask all those who want to go first and get moving to wait, or wait their turn.
4. We give remedial time and attention to all those who can't meet expectations for successful completion of the change in order to push them up to the standard.

These habits are worst when applied to changes that are self-directing or employee-led. They immediately show the employees that those words are buzzwords without concrete meaning. Many an Agile implementation has failed through this type of hypocritical centrally directed self-direction.

• • •

Change Tactic—Providing a tower of support is easier than it sounds. Towers of support are accessible platforms that anyone can access to help them reach toward your change as soon as and as far as possible.

Towers of support can be as simple as setting up a site or volunteer list where people who are excited can get involved. Here, the *Field of Dreams* movie saying is true:

> If you build it, they will come.

If the change goal is to build a new organizational capability, a tower of support would create on-demand training and make it accessible to a wide range of people right away. That allows those early adopters to move fast and test your training. Those who would fast follow then see the results of a system that works and hear about the benefits from the early adopters.

It is much easier for the early adopters to reveal themselves this way than a change team trying to guess which groups need or want the training first or will be the best change advocates.

Watch for or seek the employees who run toward and climb the tower of support tactics, going above and beyond the change request.

If the ask is for employees to mentor new employees, seek those who are already mentoring, and ask what you could put in place that would help them and others mentor more. This partnership action will produce better results than setting a rule for mentoring that you apply equally to all mentors and non-mentors consistently.

• • •

Once upon a time, I led a global Agile community building effort. My job was to find and connect Agile leaders at global worksites. When I took the role, I inherited a marquee tower of support tactic: a weekly Agile coach call. Each week, our team hosted a one-hour conversation where coaches could call in and get their questions answered—not by us but by other Agile coaches.

Who did we invite? Anyone who wanted to call in.

It was a powerful forum for finding those who self-identified as Agile coaches, who would invest the hour in the community and their own learning, and who, if we asked, would lead Agile efforts at their local site. Simple forums like the Agile coach call are great towers of support we can build in order for our change agents to reveal themselves and get the support they need to achieve the changes we all want faster and with more success.

CHANGE TACTICS
FOR PLANNING

24

HEAT UP THE TEACUP

We boil at different degrees.

—Ralph Waldo Emerson

Goal—Make the most change in the least amount of time

Status Quo Tactic—Try to boil the ocean

Change Tactic—Heat up the teacup

Why—Because focusing our energy on a small step generates the most change quickly

Status Quo Tactic—If you're Driving People, you require authority to compel your change. The assumption is that the larger the group the change applies to, the more authority I'll need to make the change happen, but also the more authority I'll have to enforce my change. In communities, this assumption leads neighborhoods to demand city changes, cities to fight for state-wide changes, and states to demand national attention. In organizations, this assumption encourages labeling all changes as corporate changes, even if only a small group of people in the company want or need the change.

This go-big strategy runs directly into the reality that to go big, you must have a big budget, lots of time, and ways to spread your message. You must have a mountain of willpower in yourself and in the distributed managers you'll count on to enforce your change.

Skeptical targets of your change will readily tell you:

You can't boil the ocean.

They're right. Remembering the Change Agent's Motto (I will do what I can, with what I have, where I am), you're likely not capable enough with large enough resources or powerfully positioned enough to make a change of that scale happen quickly. That's the fact. The compounding fact is that no one is actually skilled, endowed, and positioned to get vast groups of people to change quickly under the threat of compulsion or reward. The times in history where rapid radical change happened against the will of the people were followed by carnage and destruction, not a new utopia.

We don't need to bring these damages into our organizations, yet we do. We fight for this to be a corporate effort and spend most of our time courting the people with position or resources instead of actually working on or role-modeling our change.

Talk of corporate-wide or culture change leaves your change bloated and people confused and frustrated, and you are no farther toward your goal than you were when you began.

If I only have this much heat energy that I can apply to this amount of water, then I will never get the ocean up to 212 degrees Fahrenheit. But if

I have this much energy and a teacup (a small group of people sized to my amount of energy), then maybe I have a chance at success.

I can try. And I can put all my energy into this change. I can focus on what I can learn from trying to heat up this teacup.

I have found people who say:

We need to change the way we run meetings in my organization.

Great! How are your meetings run for your staff?

Well, that's not the point.

Yes, it is.

What if you run five meetings a week and all your meetings don't start on time, don't end on time, don't have an agenda, don't have meeting minutes, and you want to go tell 6,000 people that all their meetings should start on time, end on time, and have agendas and minutes. How well is that going to work?

People will spend time on how to get 6,000 people doing what they don't do themselves. And we are all guilty of this from time to time. Do as I say, not as I do.

I once worked with an organization that launched a Better Meetings Initiative. Pursuing a "boil-the-ocean" strategy, the change team told the 1,500 people simultaneously to improve their meetings. After six months, the organization disbanded the initiative. No meetings improved, not even those of the senior leadership team.

• • •

Change Tactic—Chances are good that the change you seek will be valuable for your entire organization, but you only see that value if you can win the organization to willingly adopt the change. They must be willing because only the things done freely ever sustain.

Many organizations have learned this lesson repeatedly during the pandemic-induced lockdowns in 2020. Those people in the organization who were enrolled personally in doing excellent work continued to do excellent work. And the conscripts' standards declined.

The Driving Change heat-up-the-teacup strategy for improving meetings starts with the leader improving their meetings, starting with their staff meeting. From there the leader expands their improved meeting behaviors to all the meetings they lead or takes part in by working with those meeting leaders to rise to their standard. From there, the leader encourages their staff to follow their example or reveal obstacles that prevent them from improving their meeting too.

With this heat-up-the-teacup strategy, you will see results of better meetings immediately, and those positive results will spread. There's no need for posters or campaigns, just leaders improving their organization through role modeling.

SHRINK THE CHANGE

Once we overcome our fear of being tiny,
we find ourselves on the threshold of a vast and awesome Universe
that utterly dwarfs
— in time, in space, and in potential —
the tidy anthropocentric proscenium of our ancestors.

—*Carl Sagan, The Pale Blue Dot*

Goal–Create force to propel the change forward

Status Quo Tactic–Frame the change as universal to give it mass

Change Tactic–Shrink the change to create maximum acceleration

Why–Because a smaller change is easier to get and keep moving

Status Quo Tactic—From physics, we know that force equals mass times acceleration. F = m*a

Mass—that's what we need. This assumption drives us to want to start all changes as corporate changes, national changes, and industry changes. First, we assume the change must be big. Then we assume we need a big authority to compel it—the maximum ability to Drive People.

We use this status quo approach because we assume:

1. If it is big, it'll be easier to get time to talk about the change in company forums or organization communications.
2. People won't pay attention to it unless it is big and being pushed by someone big.
3. We can only get system improvement if we improve it all end-to-end.

There are many problems that come with making the change universal. Here's a short list:

1. It delays the start as you lobby for the top official to endorse and enforce your change.
2. It forces you to make the change as generic as possible so it applies to the widest group as possible. "All system administrators in IT need to log in to the system at least once a month to confirm a certain field" becomes "we must all care about data quality."
3. People can't find a role model doing the change. Then they can't see how to incorporate the change into their lives. So they don't act until forced.
4. The change manager communicates again and again to get attention and push for action. That usually means the messages shift from encouraging and informative to demanding and threatening.
5. Paradoxically, just when the change manager is trying to demand more time and attention from the senior leaders and communications people to push the message onto the people,

the leaders and communicators lose interest because they think, "I already did that," and "they should know by now."

• • •

Change Tactic—An alternative to increase the force for the change is to focus on getting the most acceleration as soon as possible. A big acceleration multiplied by a small but growing mass will produce change momentum much faster.

This tactic relies on these assumptions:

1. There are very few people who need to change their daily, weekly, or monthly behavior to create a successful change.
2. If there are many people who need to act differently in order for the change to sustain, I'm more likely to win the majority by first winning some early adopters and leveraging them to spread the change message.
3. We can move faster if we have a small group that takes action now and grows from there versus waiting to get top leadership approval.
4. Much of the power in a change is in adapting the processes and structures (the infrastructure) and the rewards and recognition before asking people to change their ways. Said another way, we will move faster if we focus on back-end change before we move to front-end change.
5. Minor changes don't improve system performance, but certain minor changes at key bottlenecks or control points can radically improve system performance.

Those assumptions produce these results:

1. You can make progress your first day because if you're Driving Change, there is certainly at least one thing you can do differently today to make your change happen.
2. As you build partnerships with others who want to make the change happen and will do something with what they have

where they are, you'll gather a list of wins that are proof that the change is real; you commit, and progress is possible. People like to associate with winners.

3. You'll be looking for ways to add others to your effort, but only if by adding them you also get momentum. They have access to budget funds, and they have special knowledge. The audience you are trying to reach trusts them.

4. When you are ready to grow from the few to the more and eventually to the many, you will have battle-tested your change. That is at the core of the iterative, user-focused, demo-driven Agile development cycle—do what I can do this week, show it to the user, partner to improve by getting feedback, and repeat.

5. Rather than sitting behind an enormous obstacle and waiting for a senior leader to move it, you'll be small enough to design a path around it for now. It's much easier to get an exception for 10 people to follow a new rule than it is to get a corporate rule changed. Try for the simple and specific, and you'll keep up your momentum.

6. You will shock people because you changed so much with only what they see as "small tweaks" to the system.

So the steps are simple:

1. Start with you, and create your first win.
2. Find a first partner, and create your first win together.
3. Expand from there, watching for the smallest place to make the biggest impact and the smallest group of people who will add more acceleration than mass to your change.

Experiment and learn your way forward. The growing force for change will surprise you.

• • •

The smallest unit of change is one person doing one thing. I've started many changes by telling someone that I tried something and it worked.

Then that person tried it, and we added another and another after that until the change took off.

If you've ever read a book and told a friend about it, you've shrunk a change and started something new. If you've ever tried a new software tool and shared how much it helped you with a colleague, you've shrunk a change and started something new. What's your example of something you tried, succeeded with, and shared? That's you successfully doing this change tactic.

26

GIVE IT A TITLE
(NOT A NAME)

Charm'd with the foolish whistling of a name.

—*Abraham Cowley*

Goal—Name the change so it sustains

Status Quo Tactic—Name the change after the person
who is Driving People

Change Tactic—Give the change a title that
distinguishes it from others

Why—Because change with a title can sustain even as
the people behind it fade

Status Quo Tactic—It's [fill in the blank]'s change. We leader-label the change. We name it. We give it their name.

How is that helping us?

My quick answer:

It's not.

It's hurting our change.

When we don't package the change in all kinds of spin and polish like Quality 4.0, or Back to Basics, we give changes the name of the executive or the department that is driving the people to change. This person or organization is the well from which all orders flow.

Many people see this personalization of a change as a good thing. They say it shows ownership. And it does, but the worst kind of status quo ownership.

What [fill-in-the-blank's change] says to the organization is that [fill-in-the-blank] has self-determined to make themselves lord of a portion of your life. And worse, they have delegated this right down several levels to a mid-level team to create a spreadsheet of orders for you to follow *or else*. Even with a positive-aspirational-sounding wrapper of Quality 4.0, we all still know what is underneath—power and intimidation.

And it's fragile power and intimidation. Though naming the change after the leader is the status quo in some organizations, staying the leader for long isn't status quo anymore for most organizations. Most top leaders in organizations change companies frequently and leadership roles even more often. Hence, the likelihood that a Head of Quality will still be the Head of Quality in 18 months is low. So why should I complete all this extra work that was ordered by the Head of Quality when they won't even be here to see if I do it or not? But I will be here, and I will have to suffer the consequences of my choice to comply with the change (which usually means some other part of my job suffers) or my choice to not comply (which usually means short-term pain of being tattled on for non-compliance). I think I'll take my chances with the tattling. I'm sure many of you have made the same calculation.

Even if you meant calling it [fill-in-the-blank's change] in the best possible light with [fill-in-the-blank] actually willing to Drive Change (choose the change for themselves and help others choose it too), then this name of [fill-in-the-blank's change] quickly becomes thinking of the change as [fill-in-the-blank's] baby. Now, if I had honest concerns about the change, I would not speak up and offer them. Why not? We know to be polite and not insult someone's baby. As a friend and I once reflected on, calling it their baby means it possesses some of them, their genetic material, a vital part of who they are. The trauma to someone who is attacked for who they are by attacking their change "baby" isn't something any of us want to inflict or receive.

• • •

Change Tactic—When we Drive Change, we say we choose *the change* for ourselves and clear the obstacles for others to choose it too. Giving *the change* a title means describing it to yourself and others succinctly enough that I know what I mean, and you know what I mean by it.

At its best, the title should be something practical, deliberate, descriptive, and devoid of flourish or sympathetic flair.

2021 People Team

[Fill-in-the-company-name] Cyber-Risk Reduction Program

Playground Improvement Project

The title is an umbrella term for the work you'll be doing underneath it to accomplish the Concrete Goal(s) you've set. This descriptive and goal-focused title eliminates the flavor-of-the-month feel and eliminates the "just-do-it-for-fill-in-the-blank" sentiment.

With a title, the change doesn't have to mirror or mimic the tendencies of the leader supporting it. In fact, when the typical focus of the leader and the descriptive title aren't well-aligned, it triggers much more interest. For example, a finance leader advocating for a cyber-risk reduction program or a human resources vice president frequently talking about product quality gives the project a wider, more permanent presentation to the organization. It appears more something that all of us should have been doing well before today, and these leaders are just some people who commit to making it happen. It's also okay to have an obvious benefit you get from the change as the change leader, but the more we see the change as *our* change versus *your* change or *my* change, the more attention, support, and sustainment you'll get.

When you're good at Driving Change, you'll have a lot of success. That success will cause many people to want to name changes after you, sometimes during the change and sometimes after the fact. Resist the urge to accept this honorific. Though it is well-meaning, it accidentally reinforces the practice of leader-labeling change and perpetuates more of the negatives we just outlined than it produces positive results.

We can help people shift this habit by replying to their naming of it as our change by saying something like this:

> I'm honored that you would want to think of this change and me so closely as to call it my change.
>
> I did pour and am pouring a lot of myself into it.
>
> But I'd rather you think about it as the organization's, company's, or community's change.
>
> This change is vital for us, and I'm just the one lucky enough to get to lead it.
>
> So again, thank you for your kindness, but it will help us sustain the change together if we call it by its official title instead of my change.

First, **Un-Name the Change.** Find as many names for the change as you can. To do this is as simple as asking the people involved in and around the change two questions and writing their answers until you think you have an exhaustive enough list.

Here are the two simple questions:

1. What do I call it?
2. What do others call it?

Next, **Give the Change a Title.** Look to the Concrete Goal and the value for the organization for grand titles. If you revisit the need in each time period, then much like Netflix shows have seasons and episodes, your change will have yearly and quarterly installments.

1. Quality Program 2021
2. Summer Diversity and Inclusion Effort
3. Corporate Cyber-Security Project
4. Bremerton Beyond Accessible Playground Project at Evergreen Rotary Park
5. Workplace of the Future Initiative

Note: If a location or organization is a focusing feature, then include it as long as all those affected by or included in the change are part of the location or organization mentioned. Avoid calling the change something like the IT Cybersecurity Project if you intend to influence the whole corporation with it because the title suggests that it either only applies to IT or it is IT that is going to drive the people of the organization to obey IT or else. The alternative is if your change is about improving IT employee recruiting, then titling the change 2021 IT Recruiting Improvement Project is very helpful.

Then, **Dampen Any Leader-Labeling.** When you hear, "Oh, that's Paula's change," calmly correct people.

The operational excellence project is important for the entire organization.

We are grateful for Paula's support, but this isn't her change.

The project is our change that she supports.

27

CREATE A DIFFERENT FUTURE

During the bombing raids of World War II, thousands of children were orphaned and left to starve. The fortunate ones were rescued and placed in refugee camps where they received food and good care. But many of these children who had lost so much could not sleep at night. They feared waking up to find themselves once again homeless and without food. Nothing seemed to reassure them.

Finally, someone hit upon the idea of giving each child a piece of bread to hold at bedtime. Holding their bread, these children could finally sleep in peace. All through the night the bread reminded them, "Today I ate and I will eat again tomorrow."

—*Story told in* Sleeping with Bread: Holding What Gives You Life *by Dennis, Sheila, and Matthew Linn*

Goal—Create hope that the future will differ from the past

Status Quo Tactic—Declare that the future will be different "just because"

Change Tactic—Create a different future through our words and actions

Why—Because we must act our way into the future that we want

Status Quo Tactic—If we've spent years in organizations, we may feel like Bill Murray in the movie *Groundhog Day*, continually reliving the same day, unable to move forward.

Each year, the budget cycle comes and goes. Each year, the strategic planning happens—we form teams to meet, plan, and then collapse.

After a few years, we would be correct to assume that the future won't be any different from the past unless something happens. The problem is that we assume that what must be different in the future is someone else.

> If only I had the power to make Person A different, I could make a new future.

> If only I had control over organization B, things would be different.

But that power or control never comes, or worse, we get the power or control and it doesn't actually change anything.

And the sun rises, and the sun sets, and everything is the same.

Then a new challenge—maybe an existential problem—faces our organization, and we feel powerless to do anything other than declare that this time it will be different when we do not know how it will be different.

Rinse.
Repeat.
Sigh.
Sigh again.

• • •

Change Tactic—In our large organizations, the bread in our hands is our hope in an exciting, better future. We create and offer that bread to others through our willingness to step forward and lead transformations that we and others can choose for ourselves.

In 2018, the Gallup organization found that if employees say they feel enthusiastic about the future, then 69% are engaged with their work. In contrast, only 1% are engaged with their work if they don't have that enthusiasm.

According to Gallup and stated in the article "Making Hope a Business Strategy," 14% of workplace productivity comes from an employee's sense of hope in the future. They define hope as "the belief that things could be better and that you can make them better." That fits well with Driving Change. When you believe you can take action to create a different future than the past, you are role modeling hope and spreading hope in a time when everyone needs a little more of it.

A tangible way to amplify the hope your role modeling provides is to build an alternative timeline to show others how you see the future differing from the past. Making it visual and concrete allows others to see the vision for the future instead of just hearing you talk about it.

When you take the time to describe that alternative timeline, you're clarifying your own thinking and allowing others a hopeful place to meet you. They can bring their hope and join it to yours by adding to your timeline and testing your assumptions. Let the optimists and pessimists around you see the timeline. Let them comment. Let them battle-test it. Use the conversation to spread the hope and enroll others in it.

THE ALTERNATIVE TIMELINE BUILD PLAN

Divide a piece of paper into three sections and two columns:

	Previous Attempts	*This Attempt*
Past		
Present		
Future		

Fill in the key aspects of previous attempts at a change in the Previous Attempts column.

Past: What did you think about the past last time? Did you focus only on the best things of the last attempt, or were you honest about the challenges you faced before? (I find organizations gloss over the unpleasant aspects of the previous attempt at change and want to paint a rosier picture of their past efforts, especially if the same senior leaders led several attempts at the change.)

Present: How did you act during the change? Did you Drive People or Drive Change? Who did you include or leave out? How clear were you with the goal and how people could get involved versus just comply?

Future: What were you saying about the future last time? How aspirational did you try to paint it while you were trying to win people to change? Did any of the promises you made about the future materialize? (If not, those are likely now change scars as you try this effort again.)

Now sketch your current change in the This Attempt column.

Past: What can you honestly share about what you did and didn't do last time? The more truthful and transparent you can be about your own errors, the more this timeline will win the attention of your audience. If the leader or a technology limits you, say so. Has that changed this time? If so, celebrate that in the Present row. What problems did you find in the solutions or in implementing those solutions?

Present: What are you doing differently this time that stands out? What aspects of your change do you want to highlight? Are you Driving Change instead of Driving People? Are you including more people in the change's design? How are you addressing concerns or problems from the past in how you are acting today?

Future: What can you say about the future that you are working to make true? These should be things you can control creating and things you need help to make happen.

28
SPEED UP THE PACE

If you want to accelerate change,
you have to compress the cycle time of your difficult conversations.

—Tanner Corbridge, Propeller: Accelerating Change by Getting
Accountability Right

Goal—To speed up the completion of the change

Status Quo Tactic—Let every change progress at your standard pace

Change Tactic—Speed up the pace of change

Why—Because we speed up change when we speed up

Status Quo Tactic—There are a few questions that are likely easy to answer if you stop to think about them.

How fast does a change start in your organization?

Then how quickly do you make progress?

And what's the cadence you used to make that progress?

In most organizations, it takes teams about three months to get through the forming and storming phases of team development. Senior leaders usually expect a plan by the end of the first quarter. It can sometimes take longer if there is a full budget request included in team startup.

Then the team will usually meet at whatever is the typical cadence in the organization. Some organizations have a weekly meeting cadence for most changes. Others are bi-weekly or monthly. I once worked with a team that wanted to speed up their results but insisted that they could only meet quarterly because "that's just how we do it here."

If the rate of change in your industry has sped up and your competitors are delivering changes and results faster, is your standard pace fast enough anymore?

•••

Change Tactic—The pace you set must depend on the results you need and the time you must finish within. If you are trying to catch up or pass a competitor, you can't allow yourself to assume you have years to catch up to where they were five years ago. Time travel like that isn't possible.

Technology today allows us to make both rapid, aligned progress and continuous asynchronous progress. You can meet weekly and communicate continuously as you learn and progress. There is so much we can do together faster if only we try.

Meeting frequency need no longer be the progress marker. The team meeting cadence acts like the drumbeat that sets the pace for everything else.

So choose your meeting frequency so you carefully align it to the pace you need. If you need something done within the next five years, monthly may be good enough, but if you need something complete by the end of the year, monthly meetings won't help you speed up.

Then set your team behaviors (how we will collaborate or work independently) to support that cadence so each meeting is a celebration of progress, not just a point on the calendar where we all stop and think about the project again.

Besides the meeting frequency, you can also shrink much of the team startup time by following a few quick tips:

1. Only staff your team with volunteers. Don't accept even one conscript. This will be hard because you'll think, "But that person would be an immense help." And you're right. They would be an immense help, but only if they want to be an immense help. If they don't, it is fine to ask them a question here or there, but don't make them join your team. They will just slow you down.

2. Set a Concrete Goal—just one. If you do that to start, you can gather some quick alignment and a path for action without ensuring you know and document every single detail.

3. Plan to learn a lot before you create your plan to finish. That learning will speed up your understanding of the problem, solution space, potential advocates, and essential settlers to win. Quick actions based on what you've learned helps you gather your first quick wins and generate early momentum, which will sustain you as you push into the rough obstacle-strewn portions of your change path.

4. Do not demand a budget up front. See Tactic 37—Make Stone Soup for how to move fast and build as you go.

5. Set your team and individual Authorization Tiers (see Tactic 50—Assess Trust) so each of you and all of you together know who can take what action when, and who needs to check and ask before proceeding. That will save you messes to clean up or prevent you from missing opportunities to make faster progress.

• • •

It is okay to vary your frequency of meetings throughout the course of a change effort. I've coached teams that met daily at the start until they knew what they were going to do and had gathered all the quick learning they needed to orient themselves to the problem and potential solutions. Once they each knew what tasks they could do to advance the project, the team gathered together weekly but kept in touch electronically.

Setting the frequency of meetings to the pace we are running at the moment is the right answer. You can help a lot of teams go faster if when you hear:

We need to hurry.

Let's meet monthly.

You suggest:

I think I have a better way.

29
FROM
CHANGE WATERFALL
TO
CHANGE AGILITY

*The purpose of development projects is to deliver what the
customer needs, at the time he needs it,
to create substantially greater value than the cost of development
and to enable customer success.*

*—Niels Malotaux, How Quality Is Assured by Evolutionary
Methods*

Goal—Complete the change implementation phase
quickly

Status Quo Tactic—Wait until the launch to start the
change implementation work

Change Tactic—Build the change implementation into
the total project in iterations

Why—To learn sooner how to implement faster later

Status Quo Tactic—For many organizations, change is still the thing you do once you've issued a policy, shipped a product, or pushed code to production. We can borrow the name from the old way of project planning and label this status quo **Change Waterfall**, where all the change falls onto the organization or customers after all the work of readying for it is complete.

When we save the change work until the end, it pushes us to make the change big and load it with a bang to get attention quickly. We shove it on people quickly and encourage them to hurry and get onboard. We expect people who just hear about a change to have the same knowledge and enthusiasm as people who've been working on the change for months or years. That rarely happens.

There are many problems with this approach, but the biggest problem from the project team perspective is that the project team is at their most exhausted at the exact time this Change Waterfall approach calls for high energy to lure others toward the change.

The project team's exhaustion quickly leads to exasperation.

Why don't they get it yet?

Just make them do it.

Sadly, I've seen project leaders who used Driving Change to energize themselves and the change team throughout the project development switch back to—and double down on—Driving People when they hit the Change Waterfall step, pulling out every tool of coercion and threat just to get the change done.

When we see the change implementation as the post-project work, we struggle to sustain our momentum and kindness toward others. We get the worst of waterfall planning—big bet assumptions, hard pushes, and easy defeat. Even if you got to the win of launch, the happy-face flag you were flying at the win quickly falls as you drop back to the low energy of Driving People. And the results you'd hoped for fall with that flag.

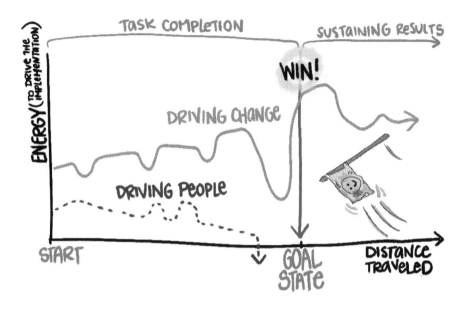

Change Paths graph from Everyone Is a Change Agent

• • •

Change Tactic—We can see the change implementation, the sustaining of our results, as part of the total flow of our work. Even better, we can build in as much learning about what we need to succeed early in our project by practicing what I like to call **Change Agility**.

Much like Agile, which builds fast cycles of customer learning into designing the product, Change Agility is the tactic of building cycles of learning about usability and change obstacles into the product or process design cycles so we can design the product or process for easy use and implementation.

Through frequent interactions with the customers of the product or process, we can learn what obstacles will keep them from adopting our change. These obstacles are typically outside the change team's authority, so the obstacles will take time to remove because the change team will have to work with others to remove them.

For example, many changes benefit if organizational metrics shift when the new change launches because the change expected new behaviors, and the metrics need to measure and reward those new behaviors. Using Change Agility, the project team works to shift the organizational metrics in parallel to prepping the change to launch.

Like Agile design, these early cycles of focusing on the change implementation with the target audiences of customers allow you to improve the design of the product or process so the greatest number of people can adopt the change as quickly as possible. After all, if we weren't trying to improve the value and success for the customer, then why are we doing the project at all? Great engineering or process design isn't enough. We must get the change implemented to get any value. And we are more likely to succeed at that if we try some Change Agility.

Using Change Agility over the years, I've had a lot of what I call if-then conversations. Design disciplines have similar conversations with various names. The whole point of these conversations is to test your assumptions and learn the perspective and experience of your target audience.

You don't have to take the audience anything finished. You can show them a sketch of the new process or a new prototype of the project. You're eager to hear any impressions, conflicts, concerns, obstacles, high points, and more. If you listen and act on what you hear, your change path will be smoother and faster every time.

• • •

Once upon a time, I was implementing an alternative method for releasing and tracking work in an engineering organization. I had assumed, based on a lot of study and planning, that the new process would transform our results. Practicing Change Waterfall, I waited until we launched the project before learning all the conflicts the new process created in the system. The metrics were rewarding the old behaviors, not the new. The computer systems and reports still pushed the engineers back to the old way of doing things. I had to scramble to fix the conflicts quickly. My rushing about and the conflicts between the new process and the old way gave people the impression that I hadn't thought out the new process very well or that it didn't work. Neither of those claims was true, but it is easy to see why people would think that.

After that experience, I vowed to use Change Agility and as early as possible watch for and work to fix implementation risks. If I cared enough to invest weeks and months of my life into this change, then I cared enough to learn early what would endanger my change's success. You will never find all the change risks before you launch the change, but you can mitigate many and help your change implement quickly and successfully.

CHANGE AGILITY QUICK QUESTIONS

1. How can I test the implementation of this change as soon as possible? If I can't test it all, can I break it down or chunk it out so I can test a portion of it? See Tactic 24—Heat Up the Teacup for encouragement.
2. What simple questions can I ask my target audience(s) to ensure I've uncovered the obstacles in the product or process design or in the wider environment that will make it hard to implement this process or use this product?
3. What actions can I take as soon as possible to remove or mitigate those obstacles?

30
A HEALTHY DOSE OF CHANGE DESIGN

When a device as simple as a door
has to come with an instruction manual
—even a one-word manual—
then it is a failure,
poorly designed.

—Don Norman

Goal—A beautifully designed change

Status Quo Tactic—Wait until implementation to worry
about the change design

Change Tactic—Include a healthy dose of change
design throughout

Why—Because we must build in beautiful design, not
superficially try to apply it

Status Quo Tactic—When we wait to look for problems with change implementation, we are too late to correct the problems. Our poor change design forces us to Drive People, pushing them to live with or power through the problems and adopt a change that is ill fitted for their needs.

Worse, there is a sad assumption that if we just communicate, train, or market the change to people more, more loudly, and stronger, we will win them to our poor design through sheer force and repetition. This approach is worse than flawed; it is insulting. It degrades us and them.

Twenty years ago, everyone assumed that training was needed before anyone could implement a change. Then we changed our expectations when applications on our smartphones and the cloud embedded teaching for how to use it in the design or through small callouts to draw our attention to additional features. None of us have taken "How to Order on Amazon" training because it is in their best interests to make it as easy as possible for us to order. That thinking needs to be injected into our change designs.

If we think of our change like a computer accessory, the easy design feature to check is whether the accessory has connected to and positively interacts with the rest of the organizational system, much like a webcam plugs into a laptop via a USB port. Too many changes require elaborate adapters to be built by the change leader after others already designed the change and launched it to the organization. We know in our own lives that we use any computer accessory that requires an adapter much less than if it has a standard connection. It is the same with change.

• • •

Change Tactic—In our daily lives, we see examples of good design enabling change to flow. We adopt new applications, new platforms, and new habits easily when they are effective and designed to spread. We share on nearly every platform we use today, except in our corporate changes, which almost never have a way to share our excitement and get others involved.

When we design for adoption and use from the beginning, we reduce the future pains of resistance and poor adoption. We lower the need for attention-draining change activities such as training or continuous communication and marketing.

Design includes user experience and implementation. We need to think about more than just what the fresh change does and also what it replaces and how it interacts with the other aspects of the organization that weren't considered.

Design your change for ease of use and compatibility, or change the surrounding systems to make them compatible with the change. Embed your change in another change, or launch them together. Design sustains long after the energy to force a change dissipates. Grand design doesn't just sustain; it spreads. Make grand change design your goal.

• • •

People often know roughly what accessible play is. Ramps. Modified swings. But beyond accessible play is something different.

Beyond Accessible Play is a design choice to design past the laws that require certain accessible features to a playground that exceed the needs of all children so there are truly no barriers to play. When Rebekah Uhtoff, the Bremerton Beyond Accessible Play vice-president and design chair, and I designed the playground for Evergreen Rotary Park, there were no Beyond Accessible Play design standards. We thought deeply and intentionally about every feature, every color, every experience, and every trade-off. The resulting playground is 9,000 square feet of wonder that delivers play experiences to children without barriers. They don't have to notice the design because it never gets in their way. They just get to enjoy it. That's the power of change design.

Again, as mentioned in Tactic 3—Break Free from the Power Paradox, you can see the playground yourself by visiting Evergreen Rotary Park in Bremerton, Washington, or watching this video that was recorded at the playground's grand opening: https://tinyurl.com/SoAllMayPlay

Since the playground opened, playground use at that park has increased sevenfold. Fun fact: you can measure playground usage by how often the maintenance team must replenish toilet paper in the bathrooms. Before the playground opened, the old playground only drew enough people to require the toilet paper to be replenished once a week. After the playground opened, they had to replenish it once a day.

SIMPLE CHANGE DESIGN THOUGHT PROMPTS

Design is a rich and vital discipline that complements change beautifully. If you are unfamiliar with design principles and methods, I strongly encourage you to at least dip your toe into the warm lake of design knowledge. Don Norman's *Design of Everyday Things* is a wonderful starting point.

For our needs here, these simple change design thought prompts get you thinking about how you might immediately improve your change design. (Huge thanks to my friend and colleague Jaye Matthews, user experience expert, for contributing to this tactic.)

Stay user-centered: It's not about you; it's about them.

Who needs to do what?

- How can you make it easy for them to do that?
- What will get in their way of doing that? What are their obstacles?
- What other factors will influence them in doing that? (i.e., competing metrics, conflicting priorities)

What's in it for them?

- What benefit will they get if they do what you want them to do?
- What enjoyment will increase?
- What pain will decrease?

What do they need to be successful?

- Knowledge?
- Equipment?

- Connections?

What can you build to show them the new?

- As-is and to-be maps
- System diagrams
- Organizational charts
- Metrics displays
- User interfaces

31
DESIGN FOR THE EARLY MAJORITY

Catering to the passionate is exactly what you should do.

—*Seth Godin*

Goal—Design the change so it spreads and sustains

Status Quo Tactic—Design for the laggards so they get on board eventually

Change Tactic—Design for the early majority to ensure they get on board quickly

Why—Because the early majority proves a change is here to stay

Status Quo Tactic—We assume we need to design our change to include everyone's concerns so everyone will get on board eventually. When we act on this assumption, we grant leverage over the change design to a group that will slow down our change: laggards.

Laggards, as defined by Everett M. Rogers in his 1962 book *Diffusion of Innovation,* are:

> the last in a social system to adopt an innovation....
> The point of reference for the laggard is the past....
> Laggards suspect innovations and change agents.

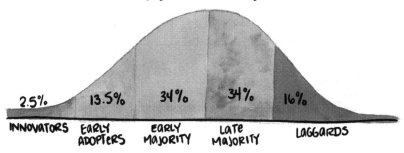

When you design to include the laggards, what you end up with is incremental change or no progress. The laggard's measure of value is always what they have rather than what they could gain. When you emphasize their perspective in the change, you lose the spark that led to the change's potency and urgency. This tendency has killed many changes during their design phase. The line of regret says:

> Well, if that's all we're going to get, then what's the point of even making the change?

And there the change dies.

Yes, ideally, we would love it if the laggards got onboard quickly with the change, and yes, we would love it if the change won everyone in an organization to the change. But we can actually get a lot of good out of a change long before we have everyone onboard.

When we design for the laggard, we create a change that isn't interesting enough to spark the interest of the other groups that Rogers mentions in his model—the Innovators, Early Adopters, Early Majority and Late Majority. So to win the last few with this tactic, we sacrifice the first four groups and the entire change with it.

• • •

Change Tactic—You will need a large group of people to get onboard willingly and quickly with your change in order to spread and sustain the change. But how large is large enough?

If you target your design to win what Rogers calls the early majority, then you're likely to gain enough momentum to succeed quickly and in the long term. Rogers gives us the roadmap to successfully spread our change:

> The early majority's unique location between the very early and the relatively late to adopt makes them an important link in the diffusion process.... They follow with deliberate willingness in adopting innovations but seldom lead.

Why not design for the innovators and the early adopters? Well, for organizational change, it isn't necessary to design for those two groups because chances are good that they are already doing what you're hoping to launch for the organization. They've just been waiting for the organization to catch up. Think of the people who read the Agile Manifesto in the early 2000s. They didn't need any organizational Agile effort to get them to be Agile. It's the same thing with diversity efforts. There are many people who have for years been hiring the best, regardless of race or gender. The corporate programs have only now caught up to these innovators and early adopters of equality and inclusion.

The early majority is the first large group of people you'll need to spend some time with or design effort on to win them. According to Rogers, they are one-third of your organization and need a deliberate reason to adopt your change; hence the encouragement of this tactic to design for them to make that deliberate choice as easy as possible.

$$\bullet\ \bullet\ \bullet$$

The pace of change frustrated me. I couldn't seem to design anything that a few of the conscripted team members would accept. Then I learned about Everett Rogers' *Diffusion of Innovation*. After reading the definition of laggard, it was easy to see that I had been designing to please them. And I had done something even worse. I had tied launching every part of the change to the laggards' approval.

If you've ever wanted to try a new application or a new process and someone stopped you until you could get the entire organization to agree, then you've suffered in the same double-bind.

The only thing worse than designing for the laggards is letting them gate anyone else from getting the change.

I learned my lesson. I listened to the laggards, but I didn't let them stop the momentum.

I started celebrating the innovators' and early adopters' wins with the change. Then I designed the change to win the early majority by connecting them with the early adopters and removing as many design or implementation obstacles as possible. And I let the laggards do what they most wanted to do—wait and see.

EARLY MAJORITY DESIGN

You can't design for the early majority if you can't identify who they are.

First, sort your key team members and key members of your change audience into the categories you think they most likely fit.

Innovators	Early Adopters	Early Majority	Late Majority	Laggards

Then take two parallel actions:

1. Connect your early majority with the early adopters who can give the early majority confidence that the change makes sense and they can do it.
2. Listen to and then act on the "Yes, but..." and "Yes, if..." ideas from the early majority for clues of what features you should add or obstacles you should remove to make the change easier for the early majority to adopt.

Finally, watch for progress.

1. Who is adopting the change? If you're getting success with the early majority, connect them with people in the late majority so the change can continue to spread.
2. Who isn't adopting the change? Who has stopped adopting it and reverted to the old ways? Seek to understand the reasons and obstacles behind both, and act on what you learn.

32
DESIGN FOR JOY

They're motivated by knowing that they can enjoy and improve their lives right now.

—*Alan Deutschman, Change or Die*

Goal–Create a sustainable feeling to sustain the change

Status Quo Tactic–Focus on eliminating what people fear

Change Tactic–Design for joy amidst the change

Why–Because delivering joy over fear will sustain you as well as the change

Status Quo Tactic—Many changes are fear-based—fear that the current pain will continue, fear of a future terrible event, fear of punishment or firing by a senior leader, and even fear of missing out.

To break through the noise of the day-to-day, we assume we must scare people so they will take action.

If we believe this assumption, then our job in part is to keep stoking the fear. Make sure the change audience knows how bad it is or how bad it could get. Point out what happened to the last person who didn't support the change. Warn them that they are being left behind.

At its worst, this tactic goes all the way to creating a manufactured "burning platform" situation—change or die. Daryl Conner says he never intended this use for his burning platform metaphor when he introduced it in *Managing at the Speed of Change* in 1992. Yet here we are—change or die.

There is a better way.

• • •

Change Tactic—Drive out fear.

That's Point 8 of W. Edwards Deming's 14 Points, wonderfully described in *Out of the Crisis*, originally published in 1982.

Driving out fear should be one of our top imperatives. There's enough to fear in this chaotic world today, so we don't need more in our changes.

If we stop Driving People, we stop driving in fear. That's not the same as driving out fear. To drive out fear, we actually need to fill the space that fear used to fill with something more powerful—joy.

We have an opportunity through our changes to help people find joy in their work. It is small measures for some and life-transforming for others, but everyone can get a bit of joy if we lean into this tactic. And whether it was Confucius or Mark Twain or Anonymous, the sentiment is right when we say:

Find a job you love, and you'll never work a day in your life.

What does joy in change look like?

It looks like this:

1. Checking in working code faster when you're excited to deliver the product to the world
2. Completing a new streamlined process and making it home for dinner (or in our work-from-home world, just closing the laptop for the night)
3. Solving a problem to capture a new market, save a customer, or improve results enough so all of us can get to do what we love again tomorrow

Give people the opportunity to create these moments of joy. Help them create a stream of wins throughout their week.

Focus on what we get if this works. Focus on what we can get today if we try today. Focus on what the world is waiting for, and help them bring their talent forward to deliver it. There is so much joy available. Go get it, and share it.

• • •

In 2014, I had the honor of keynoting at the Intel Agile and Lean Development Conference in Hillsboro, Oregon. One of my fellow keynote speakers was Richard Sheridan. He gave a talk called "Build a Workplace People Love—Just Add Joy." He's the author of *Joy, Inc.* and *Chief Joy Officer*. You can use his example to motivate you to improve the joy in your workplace. I hope this tactic encourages you to add joy to your changes.

You can see the video of his keynote at https://tinyurl.com/Sheridan-Joy

33

SKETCH THE SYSTEM

*A good conceptual model allows us
to predict the effects of our actions.
Without a good model, we operate by rote, blindly;
we do operations as we were told to do them;
we can't fully appreciate why, what effects to expect,
or what to do as things go wrong.
As long as things work properly, we can manage.
When things go wrong, however,
or when we come upon a novel situation,
then we need a deeper understanding of a good model.*

—Don Norman, *The Design of Everyday Things*

Goal—Reach a shared understanding with a broad audience for maximum action

Status Quo Tactic—Tell them again what you've already said, usually with more words

Change Tactic—Sketch the system for them and with them

Why—Because a picture is worth a thousand words

Status Quo Tactic—When we are creating change, we want action. Usually, the action we want is specific—in this situation, do A instead of B. We spend a lot of time drafting and perfecting communications to ensure that people understand exactly what we want them to do. Inevitably they reply:

It's not clear enough.

Frustrated, we decide to tell them again what we've already told them, but we embellish it, adding more detail, more reasoning, more authority (having their boss tell them is a common subtactic).

Again, they say:

It's not clear enough.

Now we're getting mad. We decide we must put everyone through a training session so they can't say we didn't tell them clearly enough or with enough detail. We write more and more and expect more exacting compliance to what we wrote. When we celebrate progress on the program, we point to all the activity we are doing to make the change clearer. We point to what we are doing because by that time we already realize that the change will not happen because the more we communicate, train, and market, the less the people we are trying to reach support our change and will act on our detailed instructions.

Frustrated, we blame the audience for their stubbornness and pray the leaders cancel the change so we can move on to something else.

Our flawed assumption is to assume that if only people could see what we see more clearly, we could force them to take the action we want. That leads us to paint our perspective in richer and richer details. What if the problem is that they see clearly from their perspective and we see clearly from our perspective, but we lack a common perspective on what we are trying to do together? We can fix this problem.

• • •

Change Tactic—We can sketch the system—the physical and organizational pathways and decision points vital to achieve the outcome we want—and we can share it with the audiences we are trying to reach.

When you're in a meeting and you can tell you aren't getting your meaning across, you can try this:

I see the system like this.

And if this is true, then Action A by you would produce Outcome Z.

That's what we're striving to achieve.

How do you see it?

Show the interfaces in the system. You know what you do or contribute and how you pass it downstream to someone else. Ask them what they do with it from there. Their answers have completely transformed changes.

Then what do you do with it?

Ask with humility, truly seeking to understand and not to prove them wrong. Listen to what they tell you. Paraphrase it, and diagram it back to them.

So, if I heard you correctly, you take the task instruction and send it through material kitting before you can assign it to a work crew.

And the weekly resourcing process assigns you work crews.

Do I have that right, and have I represented it correctly in this brief sketch?

Yes, you've got it.

Fantastic!

So that means if I were to get you the task instruction no later than noon on Monday, you could ask for the right work crews in time to save us both a week on our project schedule.

Would noon on Monday be soon enough?

And on and on this goes.

Now you're both looking at the flow together, finding points of change that you can partner on to get an outcome you both want.

You can imagine after reading this tactic that I am a huge fan of documented business processes. The value in having them documented, to whatever level you find is best in your organization, is not only so you can teach them to new employees faster but also so you can have a common reference point when you start a change. A bonus benefit of defining our work processes is the gathering together to review the business process, which takes us out of us-versus-them to us-against-the-waste-in-our-process.

You don't have to invest a lot to do this.

Sketch something on a digital whiteboard or even on the back of a napkin. The drawing is a means to get to a shared understanding. And you'll get to it if you sketch the system and work with it together.

34

CALIBRATE THE CHANGE
TO THE HALF-LIVES

*A credo of management ought to be
that every human endeavor has a "half-life."*

—Admiral H. G. Rickover, 1962

Goal—To build a sustainable system

Status Quo Tactic—Assume perpetual people, positions,
and processes

Change Tactic—Calibrate the change to the half-lives
of positions and tools

Why—To align the change's resiliency to the system's
volatility

Status Quo Tactic—Many organizations still Drive People, and many large organizations still design change assuming lifetime employment and perpetual processes.

Lifetime employment supported Driving People because you could use the threat of Leader A remembering you didn't get onboard fast enough with a change when Leader A considered you for promotions or opportunities in two, five, or 10 years. This threat encouraged you to worry that when Leader B looked at your performance track record in 15 years, they would see that Leader C had given you a poor rating 10 years ago because you wouldn't adopt the newest change.

Tenured colleagues quickly taught this system of lifetime coercion to new employees.

You don't want to get an "unsatisfactory" or "needs improvement."

It'll be in your record for the next 30 years.

The fear of the future is a powerful weapon.

People could design and deploy processes with all force because the assumption was that this was the last major change in this process that we would need for 10 or 20 years. So using extreme methods of force and coercion was a necessary means to create a sustainable end. This assumption rests on a deeper assumption that our core business processes shouldn't change frequently or they will distract us from our core jobs.

In 2020, according to the United States Bureau of Labor Statistics, the median tenure of all wage and salaried employees was 4.1 years. Only 30% of men and 28.1% of women had been with their employer for more than 10 years. That statistic doesn't differentiate between those who were in the same job or who have switched jobs with the same employer, so chances are good that fewer had more than 10 years of tenure in their positions.

When we contrast the 2020 statistics with 1983 statistics, we see how tenure is declining. In 1983, 39.9% of men older than 25 had more than 10 years of tenure with their employers. A 9.9% drop may not seem like much, but in that same period, the number of men 45 to 54 with more than 20 years of tenure with their employer dropped from 32.8% to 20.8%. Even more telling is that between 1983 and 2020, the median tenure of a manager dropped from 8.1 years for men and 5.3 years for women to 4.9 years for all managers. It's hard to sustain a "do this change or I'll remember it forever" tactic when half the managers will be with the company for fewer than five years.

Similarly, the half-life of a process is shrinking. When processes relied on the tenure of the employees and the life of a product to hold them in place, they could last for five, 10, or even 15 or more years relatively unchanged. Today, the tenure of employees and the duration of product life cycles are shrinking, and the rate of technology application to business needs is speeding up. These competing rates produce a need for organizations to assess and update processes repeatedly to take advantage of the latest technology in order to support the current employees and the latest products.

Taking three years to plan and implement a major change is no longer acceptable. Now, businesses are looking for rapid ways to adapt their business processes to new markets, and they need to implement it as soon as possible. The tactic of designing forever is no longer the right approach.

• • •

Change Tactic—You must calibrate the change to the half-lives of your positions and tools.

If your chief information officer is new every 18 months, don't hang your digital transformation on:

> The CIO says so.

Instead, you'll have to drive the change based on a business need and benefit to the employees today. How can you make the work easier for the salesperson today? How can you ensure a successful, rapid quarterly close for the finance controller now?

If the half-life of an employee in any position is shrinking, then you can't design the process the way John wants it or around Kim's demands. Instead, design it for a role and what anyone in that role would need. In organizations shifting from a forever-employment model to a shrinking-tenure situation, this shift is vital for long-term organizational success. We can't afford to waste years on custom solutions built around people who may not be there in two years while suboptimizing our business processes now and in the future. We must do better.

The bright spot of the shrinking tenure of employees and leaders is that the half-life of any organizational political situation is also shrinking. I'm sure that if you've been doing change for any length of time, you've heard some story about why you can't implement Change A because the leader of Business Unit B is fighting with the leader of Business Unit C and will only allow Change D or nothing.

Your first tactic in this situation should be to design the best solution that is agnostic of business unit needs and works best for the organization overall and then wait for either the leaders to get new roles or depart from the company. Chances are good that they will either switch positions or leave within 12 to 18 months.

Your enormous opportunity, given the shrinking half-lives, is to stand out by being the person who is designing processes that can both stand the test of time and adapt as technology and markets pivot. Admiral H. G. Rickover said in *Management*'s September 1979 issue that a person should act as though they "will remain in the job indefinitely." He contrasted that with the short-time occupant of a role he called the temporary custodian who is job hopping and does not consider the long-term interests.

We can design our changes so they will allow people, whoever is in the role, to fulfill the role successfully and also adapt. All we have to do is try.

35

MAKE THE FIRST STEP EASY

The baby's walking!

—*Every excited parent who sees their child's first steps*

> Goal—Get started
>
> Status Quo Tactic—Assume the first step must be full transformation
>
> Change Tactic—Make the first step as easy as possible so it happens right away
>
> Why—Because every successful journey starts with the first step

Status Quo Tactic—Most changes make the first step someone has to take as big as possible, and then we wonder why people can't make the leap. Almost no one could abandon all their old planning and execution methods and switch to Agile overnight or ignore all their old behaviors and transform into a new culture role model immediately.

When they don't make the leap, our analysis often focuses on hypothesizing what is wrong with those people that they couldn't "just get it" that they need to "get over it" and "get on with it."

Bah!

The problem isn't with them; it's with us.

We would never want done to us what we do to them. We would not and do not abandon what we've always done and switch to something else because someone somewhere told us to. We gradually shift from one way to the other, whether we are choosing the change or being forced to adopt it. Every change has steps. The only question is how big each step is.

As change leaders, we can size those steps so the most people can be their most effective in moving to the change. We can do much more for people when we don't assume the first step must be full transformation.

• • •

Change Tactic—Make the first step small and easy.

Sizing the first step to make it easy may mean celebrating people attending an event, accessing a site, following the new process one time, or sending a piece of feedback. The goal of making the step small is so you can see it and celebrate it in as many people as possible as fast as possible. If you can do this, even just a little more than you are today, you will see an improvement in the adoption of your change immediately.

Parents would never scatter Legos around their living rooms while their baby is trying to walk. We all know how impossible it is for even adults to walk in a room littered with Legos. Yet I see people do the equivalent of the Lego mess with their change implementations. We don't clear the way and help the change audience take their first small steps. We can do that, though, and we should.

Find the simple actions. Clear the way so your change audience can take those simple steps. Celebrate them when they do. Help them take the next step and then the next and then the next. Soon, they'll be running ahead, and you'll have to run just to keep up.

• • •

Years ago in a keynote about becoming a change agent, I congratulated the audience for already being change agents because they had taken their first change agent step just by attending my talk. Their colleagues hadn't signed up for the conference, cleared their calendars, protected the time, and gotten to the talk. I wanted to help them all see how far they had already come down a path to a better future. After the talk, a few people came up to me to thank me for helping them see their progress that they hadn't noticed until I pointed it out.

This is our power as change leaders, to help people see how easy it is to make progress to their new, better future. We can do that not only by helping them see their progress but also by designing the change journey so it is easy for them to take those first steps.

36

SCALE THE CHANGE

All who joy would win
Must share it,—Happiness was born a twin.

—Lord Byron, Don Juan

Goal—Achieve the most change benefit from each measure of time invested

Status Quo Tactic—Do the same thing repeatedly until you reach scale

Change Tactic—Do something once, then let it scale while you do something else

Why—Because we all have more changes than time to invest and reinvest in each one

Status Quo Tactic—Many change efforts still center on one-time, in-person, or online events to push the change forward. These one-time, time-intensive events set the pace for how fast the change can progress. These events drain the energy and capacity from the change team since they require intensive investment to yield each measure of change.

To achieve scale with this tactic requires either the dedication of a change agent or an entire team of instructors to provide these events. This demand for more resources or more time chokes the change and slows the spread. When the change calls for rapid results or global reach, we can't move fast enough.

• • •

Change Tactic—For decades, technology has allowed us to scale our impact beyond the one-on-one or small-group interaction at a synchronized time. Yet until today, most changes didn't leverage those technologies to provide rapid change at scale. From today forward, you can scale your change.

The tactic is simple. Do it once, and then share it widely.

If you give a speech, record it and share it.

If you create a training path, publish it and share it. Only schedule Q&A sessions to go deeper, and then record and share those too.

Flipped learning has been a concept in education for decades, but I rarely see it in use in organizations. With the distributed workplace now a new normal, I hope we can finally shift our training tactics to distributed flipped learning so we can make learning available to more people more often at lower costs, which will drive better outcomes.

Use your creativity. How can you do something once and then share it at scale so you can move on to doing the next thing while your change works for you and spreads for you? The time you free up and the people you reach will amaze you.

• • •

I once recorded a session on better meetings. The original session lasted one hour and included 20 people. More than 100 DVDs of the presentation were shared (yes, I know, mentioning sharing DVDs makes me old). The number of people who benefited from that one hour is orders of magnitude greater than the number in the room that day. We understand this obvious benefit of recording and sharing when we watch a video on YouTube, yet we rarely use the same technology and processes in our organizational changes. We can do so much better.

SCALE YOUR CHANGE THROUGH FLIPPED LEARNING

There are many people discussing how to best deliver distributed, asynchronous training. That kind of training is a wonderful way to recycle and scale your change. Liz Lockhart, an early reviewer and the person who wrote the Foreword for this book, shared her principles for participant-centered learning in creating powerful training to scale a change:

1. It's not about the facilitator; it's about the learner.
2. A trainer's job is to shorten the path to learning and knowledge.
3. Whoever is doing the talking is doing the learning.
4. Gone are the days of lecture; it's all about facilitation now.
5. Involve me, and I'll learn.
6. E-learning makes it possible to present content and then engage learners in a discussion or workshop to apply the knowledge versus "so what'd you learn in the video?" response. That's not where the learning really happens.
7. Partner with training leaders in your organization. Learn from their experiences, and build confidence in your training facilitation. That is key!

37

MAKE STONE SOUP

Little by little, a little becomes a lot.

—*Tanzanian proverb*

Goal—Grow fast

Status Quo Tactic—Ask for as much as possible as soon as possible

Change Tactic—Ask for as little as possible as soon as possible

Why—Because it is easier to say yes to something small right away

Status Quo Tactic—There's an assumption rampant in organizational change that seems to follow the common saying:

Go big or go home.

It encourages change leaders to ask for as much as possible from the organization as soon as possible under the assumption that if the organization delivers this huge request, then they have secured both the organization's support for the change and the means to achieve it.

Experience teaches that those two results of maximum funding are not likely. The sheer amount of work and waiting to get the maximum funding usually results in the change, even when funded, to be too late to make the difference that originally justified the large expenditure and investment.

I've seen changes that said:

We cannot begin until we have 100 people dedicated to this effort.

We must have an initial budget of a million dollars, and then we can get to work.

I've seen change teams work for a year or more to secure their funding. They calculated the request, justified the request, and staffed the request through laborious budget requests and approval processes. Even if they got a portion of the funding, the next hurdle of hiring the staff and architecting the organization produces further delays, and they won't deliver the first results until years after the project launches.

In these days of accelerating change, the delays built into this all-or-nothing tactic are self-defeating for the change. There's a better way if you want to grow quickly (and get results while you grow).

• • •

Change Tactic—First, every change starts with the same budget and resourcing—zero. It's what happens after this start that makes all the difference. While your status quo colleague gets busy building their budget request case, you can start something much more successful—make stone soup.

The old folk tale "Stone Soup" shows us the successful way to build something out of nothing.

Our tale begins with some wayward travelers arriving in a village. They are hungry, but all they have is a pot. What are they to do?

The travelers gather a bit of wood scattered about and start a fire. They draw the attention of the villagers who come out to ask:

What are you doing?

We are making stone soup.

Stone soup?

Yes, it is the latest craze. We've just been in the neighboring village, and they all loved it.

Would you like to help us make it?

Perhaps.

Very well. We will get started, and you will see how you can help.

First, I will get some water from the creek.

Now I'll add this special stone and get the water boiling.

Yes, it already smells delicious.

It would smell even better if I had a carrot or two.

Does anyone have a carrot or two to spare?

I do.

Fantastic! Thank you.

Now, it would taste all the better if we had some cabbage and potatoes.

Does anyone have any to share?

I do.

Me too.

Wonderful!

Delicious!

And this goes on until the pot is full, the soup is hardy, and it is ready for all to eat well.

Now, let us all share in this wonderful soup.

The theme is that we don't have to start with much to end up with much if we can encourage others to join us by asking them to offer what they have and want to share.

Stone soup works; you can try it today. Shrink your first request for change.

Instead of asking for full funding for your advanced degree, ask for $500 to purchase an initial course or one that would show the applicability of the degree to your job.

Don't request funding to train the entire department. Instead, ask for $50 to buy some books for a book club.

If you can't start there and show value, then don't ask for $1 million and 100 people because that will take you years to get. Getting $350 should take a week. And if someone is fighting you for more than a day over $50 in an organization where you are trying to Drive Change to improve a product or service, then they have wasted more making you wait than they would have by saying yes.

• • •

I and the many people of Bremerton Beyond Accessible Play used this stone soup tactic to go from zero dollars and an idea to building the county's first beyond accessible playground to more than $500,000 and a fully funded 9,000 square foot playground plus major park improvements.

Our first ask was for $350 dollars to buy a banner because if you are a community group, you don't really exist until you have a banner. I showed up and said:

Hi! I'm April from Bremerton Beyond Accessible Play.

Okay.

Where's your banner?

Oh, right here.

Okay.

Now you exist.

We bought the banner, and we turned that banner and the initial $350 into a movement. Two years later when we celebrated our progress at a celebration, groups were bringing us checks—checks for $2,000, $5,000, and $10,000.

We said:

Here is how much we have.

Here is what we want to do.

And here is how we are going to parley that.

We were collecting pennies and nickels in change jars at convenience stores. We were collecting $25 apiece from people to fund a square foot of our accessible surfacing, and we were collecting thousands of dollars from various organizations. Quickly over the course of three years, while working full-time and having two more children (I had two when we started the project and four by the end), we built the accessible playground at Evergreen Rotary Park in Bremerton, Washington. Since it opened, children of all abilities have continually filled this place where all can play together.

STONE SOUP WORKSHEET

1. What do I have to start the soup? (an idea, a connection, a position, a path to value)	
2. What's the first small thing I need to show I'm on my way to something bigger? • How can I make it as small of an ask as possible? • Who can I ask that will both think it is a small request and have it to give me?	

3. What is the list of asks I want to make once it works?
 	
• It's okay to not know all these answers now. As you move forward, you'll see more opportunities, but list as many as you think of. These are options right now, not actual requests to make yet.
• How specific can I get with these asks?
 	
  ◦ How much?
  ◦ Who?
  ◦ What are the conditions I might ask under?
  ◦ Are there any timing issues or opportunities? (e.g., during the budget proposal phase, within the yearly grant schedule, at the monthly meeting)	

4. How will I share the results or credit with the people who've helped me? • What celebration events can I create? (Because no one else will celebrate you, you'll need to build the events yourself.)	
5. How can I share my thanks in ways proportional to the help offered? (Beware of thank you schemes that end up more work for you—like bricks with people's names etched into them or integrated naming—because they will distract you from the change.)	

CHANGE TACTICS
FOR ACTION

FROM CONSUMPTION TO RENEWAL

*There is ... an enormous reservoir of relatively untapped genius
—that is, the capacity for exceptional accomplishment—
which existing systems of motivation have failed to reach.
Even a small penetration into this reservoir could be hugely
rewarding.*

—Saul Gellerman

Goal—Harvest the most energy from the situation and organization toward the change

Status Quo Tactic—Burn out the people and the relationships

Change Tactic—Unleash the energy inside people and in relationships to speed change

Why—Because renewable power in people and organizations sustainably fuels change

Status Quo Tactic—Driving People is a lot like running your organization like a coal-powered energy plant.

Yes, we need the energy it produces, but the process to get it is messy and wasteful, and creates long-term consequences for a wide range of people. Coal plants have low energy efficiency, with many sources citing efficiency below 40%, which means that for every unit of coal burned, only 40% of the energy turns into electricity.

This is very similar to the energy lost in Driving People.

A simple example:

We create a team of 10 conscripts to work on a change.

Initially, we start with 10 people's worth of energy. But we quickly see our energy decline.

A few people attend meetings but rarely take part.

This prompts one of the team members, usually the project manager, to redirect energy from the change to trying to get participation from the lagging team members.

Then, even when the team is meeting, we spend most of our time discussing what people outside the team must do instead of doing something ourselves. We aren't moving; we are spinning in place.

We continue to lose energy by pushing people to move, to change. That produces a lot of friction since the people we are pushing push back, resist, or respond with confusion and ask for more clarity.

In the end, there are a few people doing the change, but they were already doing the change before we asked. Everyone else is where they were before we started, or worse. The change has scarred them, and they will resist the next one even more.

This is the organizational toxic waste of Driving People.

• • •

Change Tactic—When we Drive Change, we are setting our change up like a hydroelectric dam.

We believe there is natural energy in people that they are eager to share with the system, if only we could harness it as it flows from them every day. Their potential energy is much like the potential energy in falling water that flows from mountains to the seas.

Here's our example:

We start a team with people who want to Drive Change (they have already chosen the change and are eager to clear the obstacles for others).

Then we set a Concrete Goal and start. We each run our leg of the change and bring our superpower in service to the change. We help others make small, easy steps toward the change, see their success, and join us.

We continue to direct our energy toward the change, not toward their fellow employees.

The team comes together quickly and produces a wealth of ideas of what they could do right away to advance the change.

After rapidly aligning on the list and prioritization, people are eager to step forward to lead individual efforts to act, to move the change forward, or to reach out to others to learn how to remove their obstacles so they can choose the change too.

You'll see energy unlocked in the team members. They will unlock energy stored in others as you win them to the change. That unlocks energy in the organization to move toward the change. It is a cascade. It is beautiful. It is renewable.

Since the consumption model is so engrained, it is vital to assess your current state of consumption versus renewal to help you deliberately escape the status quo and move to this change tactic. See the assessment below to support your escape.

• • •

For seven years I ran a Guiding Coalition built on Driving Change and a belief that there was an immense amount of untapped energy in our organization. Using this tactic and others, we achieved more than 75 tangible improvements and only ran on one half-time position for a Guiding Coalition Managing Director (me) and small hourly budgets of time for the participants. Each year, more than 200 people found time above and beyond their day jobs to create wonderful, powerful, necessary, long-overdue changes for their organization. I may not believe it if I hadn't lived it, but it was real, and it is repeatable.

It was a marquee example of a hydroelectric system of change: capture the energy, channel it, harness it, transmit it, and leverage it. It works.

ASSESSMENT OF CONSUMPTION VS. RENEWAL

Put an X next to the signs that apply to your change project, and then add the number of Xs in each column to see if you are more consuming than renewing your change energy.

Yes? Mark an X	Signs of Consumption	Yes? Mark an X	Signs of Renewal
	We force conscripts to take part.		Volunteers fight to join and stay involved.
	Project manager time is spent convincing team members to take part or complete their tasks.		Project managers welcome new members or new partners.
	Team meetings are spent planning what other people should do.		Team meetings are spent planning or completing work that the team will do.
	Team meetings are spent sharing the status of other people's actions.		Team meetings are spent gaining clarity and making progress.
	Others outside the team must force or threaten people to complete tasks.		We complete tasks voluntarily, and others are joining the effort voluntarily.
	Obstacles to the change grow in size and number.		We reduce obstacles to the change in size and number.
	Complexity increases through new rules and expectations.		We reduce complexity through simplification and voluntary partnerships.
	We measure progress against the time invested (i.e., three days have passed, so we have three days of progress).		We measure progress against change in the systems or organizational results.

Yes? Mark an X	Signs of Consumption	Yes? Mark an X	Signs of Renewal
	Maybe we know what is in the change for us, but we don't know what is in it for others.		We know what is in the change for us, and we help others share what is in the change for them; we try to increase both.
	Team member are mostly conscripts, forced to participate.		Team members are volunteers who feel seen, heard, and appreciated. They are psychologically safe enough to voice doubts and concerns.
	Celebrations are prohibited (or not considered) until the full change is complete, restricted in who gets the praise, and formally provided.		Celebrations are frequent, and recognition is distributed and energetically enjoyed.
	People blame each other for the things that are not going well.		People collaborate with each other to solve problems and plan next steps.
	There is not enough or no support from others to remove organizational impediments on time.		Team members and others work daily to create the change together as one team.
	There is an increase in exhaustion of team members.		There is increased energy in team members who fight to do more and go faster.
	Team members are constrained by what we have always done.		Team members are continually looking for better ways to work and improve.
	Decisions take a long time to make.		An empowered team makes informed decisions quickly and decreases the number of decisions that management must make (see Tactic 50 for how to do this).
	TOTAL		TOTAL

To move from consumption to renewal, switch from Driving People to

Driving Change and use many other tactics in this book, and you will watch your change energy rise and renew.

39
CREATE YOUR OPPORTUNITIES

Know the true value of time;
snatch, seize, and enjoy every moment of it.
No idleness, no laziness, no procrastination:
never put off till to-morrow what you can do to-day.

—*Philip Stanhope, 4th Earl of Chesterfield, Letters, December 26,*
1749

We must hurry, but the executive's calendar is full.
Let's plan for November.

—*A change leader in February*

Goal—Use events to speed up change
Status Quo Tactic—Wait for events to prompt change
Change Tactic—Intentionally create rapid opportunities to change
Why—Because change proceeds as fast as we create opportunities for it to happen

Status Quo Tactic—In planning for a change, many change leaders try to time change launches to big events in the organization—yearly sales conferences, quarterly updates, recurring product launch cycles. Many changes suffer from these delays.

Though they yell:

We must go faster!

Still, they wait.

Look at your current change plan. How much of it have you tied to events that are recurring versus timed or sequenced events to maximize your change? If you wait for events to prompt your change, that's time you're giving away unnecessarily.

In the past, besides waiting for these events to happen, we also assumed that we had to hold the events in person. That's where we would do our networking or strategic planning, have our tough conversations, or make new connections. The assumption was that we couldn't do those things virtually. Because we assumed that in person was the only way to strengthen connections and ensure we were on the right track, we thought we had to live with the delays that waiting for availability on our calendars or conference centers required. For some international events, our travel time and the recovery days from the jet lag were longer than the actual events. These assumptions and the tactics to live with them forced delays, exhaustion, and expenses. We assumed it was all worth it. It wasn't.

• • •

Change Tactic—If your change is urgent, then build momentum now so if you intercept a big event, it will be an accelerator, not a launch.

You can create opportunities to change by thinking about who you most want excited about your change and create opportunities to engage them directly or piggyback on ongoing events to introduce portions of your change.

A simple example of piggybacking is asking to be added to recurring staff meetings to share your change versus waiting for an opportunity to hold a major launch event.

Another example is starting a simple forum on your organization's internal social media to share messages and test their success. What generates the most engagement? How can you invite more people and get them to want to follow your change?

A favorite tactic, one you can borrow from a line in the hit musical *Hamilton*, is to put yourself in the "room where it happens" by creating a room for the discussion. People respond well to being invited to conversations that are both focused and open-ended; for example, "How might we quickly improve our product quality?"

As we've learned with the global pandemic, when we move past our in-person bias, we can connect with anyone anywhere at a moment's notice. Yes, the online platforms have some limitations, but often we can live with those limits or purchase our way past them. Compared to our old physical limitations, the options are endless and inexpensive.

When we create virtual opportunities, we open up opportunities for more people to get involved quickly. You can still have regional teams, but you can also add global members to any team. It will surprise you who joins a call at odd hours for them if it is about a change they are passionate about.

Flipped classrooms and asynchronous dialogue tools allow us to record a presentation once and trigger a global conversation that is convenient for local audience members. If your business follows the sun, you could have three opportunities to present and 24 hours of ongoing conversation on an online platform in just one day. That speeds up change when you contrast it to the old models of global in-person events that typically spread out over weeks if not months to accommodate executive travel schedules.

When you shrink the request to others, from "attend my three-day event" (which really means block five days of your schedule to get here, participate, and get home) to "please join my virtual change event for one hour," you've given yourself many immediate opportunities to create change participation. While this opens up many opportunities, it also creates a wealth of chances for people to continue to waste others' time. As I watched organizations adjust to the pandemic conditions in 2020, I assumed that the cancellation of executive travel would open up a wealth of opportunities for executives to connect more deeply and more broadly with their organizations. I didn't see it.

In the 1960s, C. Northcote Parkinson coined his eponymous Parkinson's law—work expands to fit the time allowed. Here, the executive workweek free of travel didn't open things up. The time for change opportunities, if it appeared, quickly filled up with other demands.

We don't have to live with Parkinson's law. We can fight back. We can make the most of our time and others' time by creating quick opportunities of just enough time for each person to progress the change.

CREATE YOUR OPPORTUNITIES OPTIONS LIST

Replace scheduled, in-person events with a range of rapid options (many virtual) to optimize change speed and community building.

1. Record a lecture and have participants watch it beforehand so the synchronized time you're together is all workshop, question-and-answer, or discussion. This also allows people who learn differently to maximize their learning by watching it again (faster or slower) or researching the questions they would like to ask and preparing their comments or insights for the workshop.

2. Wisely expand the participant list since there is less cost to scaling participation. Beware of sending the invitation to everyone. You don't want people attending just because they got an invitation, but you also want to ensure that those with a passion for the change can attend. Many in-person events had to choose the organizational winners or losers to fit into a budget window, using arcane rules such as tenure instead of passion for the change to drive who did and didn't get to participate. With this tactic, you can also use the event as a development opportunity by inviting specific people as observers. Typically, if a person cares enough to invest their time in attending, you'll benefit from it in a direct or oblique way (e.g., they share the details of the event with someone who

turns into a key advocate because they first learned about it from their passionate colleague instead of a corporate e-mail).

3. Just as you would have done for successful in-person events, block calendars and provide agendas to enable full participation. Just as it was pointless to attend a conference only to spend a lot of time in telephone calls back to the office, a virtual event overloaded with multitasking of in and out for meetings will also be less effective.

4. Leverage breakout room capabilities of modern virtual platforms. Let people share in small groups. That was where most of the best "aha" moments and connections came from at in-person events. Asking an open-ended question of the breakout is the fastest way to get the group talking. Moderate the breakouts as you would have moderated them if they were in person. Good facilitation is even more important in cyberspace than in person.

5. It is important for people to go to virtual events as teams. Why? Because with all the demands of home and work, it is easy to skip the virtual event if you're going alone. But if my colleague Jaye is expecting me to either be in the session or debrief her afterwards, then I am more likely to show up and benefit from the experience.

I could have included many other tactics here, but rather than giving you an exhaustive and likely quickly outdated list, I'll encourage you to capture your best tactics and share them with others.

What's the tactic?	*Who will I share it with?*

40

FEEL THE MOMENTUM

Time is relative;
it's only worth depends upon what we do as it is passing.

—Albert Einstein

Goal—To speed up the change

Status Quo Tactic—Speed up relative to what the
organization thinks is fast

Change Tactic—Feel the momentum relative to others
so you can be the pacesetter

Why—Because fast is relative

Status Quo Tactic—Each organization has its own clock. Often, that organizational clock runs at a different pace than other organizations' clocks. In large, established organizations, some clocks seem to run slower than the market or their competitors. Other organizations continue to surprise us with their blazing speed. Each organization has its own **organizational time warp** when time runs differently inside versus outside the organization.

Most organizations say a change is moving "fast" or "slow" relative to the organizational clock, not the market or competition clock. That leads to projects that lag the competition but continue for quarters or years. It leads to pressure to slow down when the project appears to be moving faster than a typical effort within the company or calls to go "faster"— calls that go unanswered because organizational members don't see either how to go faster or why the extra speed is necessary.

You are in an organizational time warp if your organization misses market opportunities and slips schedules, yet you continue to hear:

Slow down!

Wait.

Not yet.

I've encountered organizations that wanted to catch up to the competition and proposed three-year plans to get caught up.

When did the competition accomplish what you had hoped to accomplish in the three years?

Oh, I'd guess about five years ago.

You likely have the same shocked look on your face now that I had then.

Organizations that think of themselves as industry leaders are often shocked when first presented with the full span of their time warp.

We can't possibly be working this hard just to be eight years behind the competition.

Yes, you are.

But you can catch up.

• • •

Change Tactic—When you help people feel the momentum, you will help them speed up their changes so your organization can be the pacesetter. Then they will speed up to beat the market and the competition.

Many authors of books about change encourage you to focus on short-term wins to build initial momentum. John Kotter emphasized this so much that he dedicated one of his eight steps to it. The emphasis on short-term wins helps you create a series of reference points the team can use to recognize their progress when, unlike an assembly line where you can watch the product move through the manufacturing or assembly process, the progress in most change is less tangible unless highlighted.

To calibrate the team to the market or competition, I encourage you to pick an aspect of the market or the competition that you can clearly date stamp; label it when it first appeared in the market or became a key habit.

For example, if you're trying to improve your buying processes inside your organization, taking several years to update your procurement systems to digitize your paper procurement process likely places you decades behind the internal processes of your competitors. If Amazon could launch a "buy now" button before 2015, why can't you jump from a paper, e-mail, or slow digital procurement process to a "buy now" platform in your company? What holds most organizations back from even having this conversation is the assumption that jumping ahead is "too fast." When I probed what "too fast" means, there is never a specific answer grounded in technical or financial details. It's more a feeling of rushing.

You can help your organization get comfortable with a speed matched to or exceeding its competition by continuing to help it see the progress in small wins and calibrate them against the market and the competition.

A word of caution: don't aspire to improve just to a benchmarked, best-in-class standard. Best in class is a polished way of saying "late second place." It's true that if your organization lags your competition in key areas, you are likely suffering some lost momentum or profit, but you will never speed up past your competition if you are waiting to see where they are and then spending months or years just to match them. You'd be better off investing your time in leaping past the competition with your internal processes or surprising the market with a product launch ahead of what was expected. You'll never do that until you embrace this tactic and speed up so you're the pacesetter.

To succeed with this tactic, I should add some key definitions that will help you determine whether you need to speed up on a known path or blaze a fresh path.

We call any big change a transformation, which implies a significant, irreversible change (think caterpillar to butterfly). That leads us to assume, much like the time warp, that if the change seems big to us, it must be a transformation. With that assumption, we make changes that are technically and operationally proven and safe into something we treat as problematic, risky, and dangerous. To lower the anxiety of transformation and help people speed up, I break transformation into two types.

Type 1 Transformation is a low-risk transformation. It is something that may be a significant, irreversible change for us, but many people have done it before, and it operates by known mechanisms. Yes, our caterpillar is becoming a butterfly, but we aren't the first caterpillar to become a butterfly.

Type 2 Transformation is path-blazing transformation. It is significant, irreversible change, and we are the first ones to attempt it. Many of the best examples of Type 2 Transformation in recent years are Tesla and Space X. They are breaking through all the time scales of how long change *should* take and what we think is possible. Update all cars to fix bugs without physically recalling any of them? Done. Land and recover a reusable booster rocket instead of abandoning a single-use booster rocket? Done.

Type 2 Transformations are industry-changing, and they are rarer than Type 1 Transformations. We can help our organizations realize how many of our changes are Type 1 Transformations and speed up today.

• • •

I'm sitting in the audience of a corporate event waiting for the announcement of a major corporate initiative.

We must do X.

And we will spend the next three years to get there.

My heart sinks. I can quickly do a web search for "when did the first company do X?" and always get an answer. That's the time stamp. That's the target we're chasing. And, we're never going to get back to a competitive advantage by spending years racing to catch up to their past.

You can time stamp all your changes. The time stamps will give you a sign of which changes to abandon and which ones to redesign to leap past the competition.

41

ELIMINATE THE TRIVIAL

... the Law of Triviality ...
the time spent on any item of the agenda
will be in inverse proportion
to the sum involved.

—C. Northcote Parkinson

Goal—Use agendas to drive action

Status Quo Tactic—Assume if it is on the agenda, it is equally vital

Change Tactic—Eliminate the trivial so you can focus on the vital decisions

Why—Because so much of the time we waste on change is on the trivial, not the vital

Status Quo Tactic—We assume that anything that is on our agenda is vital. Is it?

Famous for his eponymous Parkinson's law (work expands to fit the time allowed), Parkinson coined several other laws that are worth remembering. In 1957, he introduced us to what he called the law of triviality. It says, "The time spent on any item of the agenda will be in inverse proportion to the sum involved." This law is key to understanding the state of most change teams today.

All but the worst change teams have an agenda for their meetings. These agendas capture the key discussions and actions the team is focusing on. When these changes are small or focused on one organizational unit, we can forgive a lack of awareness of the law of triviality. But when the change is organization-wide or includes people from diverse functions or both, knowing the law and its operation is crucial.

In the essay "High Finance or the Point of Vanishing Interest," Parkinson lays out a hypothetical meeting to show his law in action. In the meeting are several decisions before the committee, including buying a nuclear reactor project for $10 million and a bike shed for $3,000, and whether to offer coffee in the break room for less than $100 per year. Parkinson, with his usual dry wit, shows that the reactor will receive little time because it is so large and so detailed that few on the committee feel qualified to question it, so they look to a few to set the discussion and go along. For the bike shed, the committee brainstorms and weighs options, and everyone can imagine a shed, the decisions that are important, and each key opinion. Debate ensues, but it is just a warmup for the most contentious topic: the coffee. Everyone understands coffee, and it is easy to have an opinion about what to offer and why. The discussion drags on, and the issue remains unresolved and is pushed to the next meeting.

Oh, how many change meetings are likely jumping into your mind right now? Key decisions are glossed over. Insignificant details are held in contention for days, weeks, and months. Sometimes large changes collapse on unimportant details and a lack of alignment. However, the consequences of a failed coffee decision are small, and the consequences for the reactor project are infinite.

Knowing the law of triviality, we can create better change meetings to drive rapid, sustainable action.

• • •

Change Tactic—Eliminate the trivial so you can focus on the vital.

The first thing you have to do to accomplish this tactic is to divide the trivial from the vital and create a third category: specialized. Each change team will have a different threshold, but here are some simple sample rules to prime you to create your own.

1. Trivial: We will not discuss incomplete items that are about an action one person or a small group will take and that don't have negative risks for the team. Reach out to the stakeholder, or research the team's solution options. Report your findings or what you learned. Don't ask to meet or learn together. Just get it done.
2. Trivial: We will not discuss items below a certain materiality level (cost or time invested). The team should act and report results.
3. Trivial: These are any status updates that will ramble when presented in person and could have been better documented and consumed in writing (i.e., in an e-mail, on a perpetual chat, submitted to be added to meeting minutes).
4. Vital: These are any actions sensitive to rapidly changing conditions. They are best discussed with the group to ensure that the situational awareness of the person taking the action is most current and holistic.
5. Vital: These are decisions that will change the Concrete Goal(s) the team is pursuing. The team needs to study materials and a list of the options before the meeting so the discussion can be constructive and fact- and data-based.
6. Specialized: These decisions or discussions require a deep or broad knowledge of a topic and thus cannot happen either quickly or superficially to achieve an effective decision or understanding of the situation.

Defend your agenda and your shared team time from the trivial, and your change will speed up.

• • •

Once upon a time, the Guiding Coalition I led had 24 active teams that needed their vital agenda items included in a bi-weekly, 55-minute meeting. To accomplish the feat of focusing that many teams on the vital, we did several things simultaneously.

First, we set the bar very high for what qualified as vital. The most vital topics were those where the team would frame to the group (usually 50 people) what they needed in order to make faster progress and ask for their input.

Then, because we couldn't have any of the people with suggestions speak in series and still get done with the agenda, we made the agenda into a feedback form where anyone in the meeting could add their suggestions, comments, or encouragements to the agenda item. Then the team would receive the summarized inputs later.

This focus and method allowed 12 teams or more to report progress and ask for help in each meeting. The remaining teams stayed off the agenda. They were teams that didn't consider any of their status updates vital enough to need agenda time. They filed their status updates in writing for others to review later.

So, in a 55-minute meeting, we updated our Guiding Coalition members and senior leaders on the amazing, concurrent progress of 24 teams.

42

FROM EVENTS TO DAILY MOMENTS

Give us this day our daily bread.

—Matthew 6:11

> Goal—To speed up the change through encounters with the change
>
> Status Quo Tactic—Create intermittent opportunities to experience the change
>
> Change Tactic—Create daily opportunities to bring the change to life
>
> Why—Because daily opportunities accelerate us to a new normal

Status Quo Tactic—Many efforts for continuous changes such as culture or quality still rely on intermittent change prompts driven by communication plans that include a mix of communication events. There may be weekly newsletters sent to inboxes or quarterly events that feature updates on the change, but the key to all these events is that they are episodic and one-way communications.

Let me tell you what I want you to hear.

Did you get that?

Let me tell you again next week.

And the week after that.

And after that.

If a person in the target audience is out of the office on the day of the event or misses the e-mail in the flood of messages in their inbox, then even though there is a regular cadence of communication from the change program, none are hitting this target audience member, and the amount of change is low.

Yes, the repetition of your telling me about the change may prompt me to remember the change, but it won't likely prompt me to action. Communications rarely motivate us to action, and intermittent experiences seldom turn into new habits. If your change needs more than moments of the new, you'll need a different tactic.

• • •

Change Tactic—Create daily opportunities to bring your change to life.

Not all changes require a daily change in behavior, but for those that do, this tactic is essential.

Successful athletes have workout streaks. Successful writers have writing streaks. Successful change agents build change streaks into their organizations. The encouragement for daily renewal is such a classical concept that it is biblical.

As many religions call their believers to daily prayer and devotion or meditation, so too should change agents like you should look for subtle and effective ways to build the change into the lives of the change audience so it becomes who they are and how they work.

Sometimes, this is as simple as giving them an affiliation they can reference daily. Years ago, we only granted Guiding Coalition membership a year at a time, and selection was very competitive. The power for change in this structure is that every day that someone could call themselves a Guiding Coalition member was a special day not to be wasted. This time span on their identity was a daily prompt to remember to Drive Change and take an action to advance their change and their change agent skills. I rarely saw time wasted.

Other times, this tactic manifests as something changed in a process or practice to allow people a daily opportunity to practice the fresh change. If you're working to create a more dialogue-based change effort, then you as a change agent can daily post topics that will spark engagement in the group and build the behavior from there. Sharing your streak and challenging others to compete with you for the longest streak of daily engagement on the chat forum is a fun way to compete and achieve a change goal. It isn't easy. And you won't always keep up your streak. But even in that "failure," there is actually progress. Why? Because we all miss a day, but few people start again once they miss. Through something like this tactic, you can role model starting again, and again, and again. The most important changes are the ones we want to live daily, and if we don't teach ourselves to keep trying again, we will never teach our organizations how to do that too.

The goal is that these daily behaviors move quickly from being what you do to who you are, or even that you stop thinking about them at all. As I'm watching my daughter learn to drive, I'm constantly reminded of the things seasoned practitioners take for granted are the things new students do only through intention. So if we want to become seasoned drivers or seasoned change agents, we need to first move into a repeated (ideally daily) set of habits, then they can become our second nature.

43

MOVE THE RESULTS INTO
THE MEETING

We don't have to wait.
We can get that done now.

—*Marta Zoglman*

Goal—Make the most progress right away

Status Quo Tactic—Make a complete list of actions to do soon

Change Tactic—Move the results into the meeting by taking quick action in the meeting

Why—Because we can do many little actions before the meeting even ends

Status Quo Tactic—The peak of effective project management is the project manager who can get the team to agree on actions they will take soon after the meeting ends and who can add the tasks to a tracker and ensure that the team completes them. Some see this as a sign of team success and shows a high-functioning team. And it is wonderful.

Just getting to that point would be fantastic.

Yes, but if you're trying to get the most done in the shortest amount of time and you want to make progress the right way, then just aspiring to the status quo of a high-performing team may not be enough.

Let's take a simple example from any high-performing team. The task: setting up a meeting with a key person to get information to advance the project.

Typically, a team member, Bob, would take the task to set up the meeting. The project manager, Sarah, would then assign Bob the task to set up the meeting in the team's task tracker. Bob would have to remember to do the task later when he had a free moment. Maybe that would be right after the meeting, or maybe it would be by the end of the day or the next day.

Simple tasks like that can lag a week from their assignment date because they are so small. They are both easily forgotten or easily postponed with the thought that it'll be easy to do it when I get time to do it. Those simple delays can add up to a lot of time lost for both short and long projects.

There must be something better we could do now to get more progress right away.

• • •

Change Tactic—Do the simple work in the meeting.

If Bob has a task to set up a meeting with Yaoz, then pause the meeting for a moment while Bob sets that meeting up, or allow Bob to work quickly on setting up the meeting while the conversation shifts to a task that another person needs to take.

If you use this tactic, then by the end of the meeting Bob's task is complete, you know when the next progress step (the meeting with Yaoz) will happen, and there is no need for Sarah to track the task.

Even better, you may find opportunities to do more in the delay between this meeting and the scheduled meeting with Yaoz.

This tactic works great in large team meetings and can be a fundamental change in one-on-one meetings. Together, you may complete several key actions or decisions during a one-hour meeting rather than spending time agreeing on what each of you will do later. That usually results in one of you e-mailing or instant messaging the other when you are doing the task because you don't remember all the details of what you agreed to. These check-ins and reminders can be very distracting for the other person, but we prioritize them because the interrupted person wants to support the progress their team member is trying to make.

• • •

Marta and I have been using this tactic for a long time. We made it our default way of working in our one-on-one meetings. We regularly pause while one person sets up a meeting or sends an instant message to someone else to ask a question. The items on our list of tasks we have to track after the meeting are nearly zero. We look forward to each of our meetings because we don't have a list of undone tasks we have to apologize for or explain away. All our projects move faster.

There's no worksheet or checklist for this tactic. All you have to do is try it. I bet you'll like it.

DON'T STALL BEHIND A NO

Don't take no for an answer.
Never submit to failure.

—*Winston Churchill*

Goal—Accelerate change with support from senior leaders

Status Quo Tactic—Assume a no is a no, and halt your change

Change Tactic—Assume that any no is a misunderstanding that can easily become a yes

Why—Because misunderstandings are more common than persistent no answers

Status Quo Tactic—In many organizations there are few people who can say yes and multitudes who can say no. This is so widely true that when we hear *no*, we assume it must be authentic. We don't even check. In my experience, most of the *no* claims you hear don't come from the actual person who supposedly said *no*. Instead, you hear about the *no* from others.

A member of your team will say:

The vice president of Human Resources doesn't support this change.

And everyone will assume it must be true.

Our experience leads us to this conclusion because we've rarely heard stories of a vice president who supported a change that wasn't their change. (Tactic 26—Give It a Title (Not a Name) relates to this.)

This assumption of *no* is a natural consequence of the status quo of Driving People. The logic flows:

Someone has to order a change to support it.

I haven't heard of that vice president ordering this change.

Therefore, they must not support it.

In this logic, no one could either support or be indifferent to a change they didn't order. So until we hear differently from that vice president, our habit is to sit and wait for a *yes*. In this situation, I've seen project teams build delays into their schedules, assuming some sort of cooling-off period for the *no* they never actually heard from the vice president. They end up talking to themselves.

Let's wait a few months and revisit it.

Yeah, that sounds about right.

Okay, I'll schedule a meeting to meet again in two months.

And the delays grow and grow and grow.

• • •

Change Tactic—When we are Driving Change, we start by gathering *yes* answers. And the most important *yes* is ours.

Will I choose this change for myself?

Yes.

Then I have all I need to begin.

The next *yes* is the one you get from those who join your change. The simplest way to find them is to ask:

Do you want to join me for this change?

If yes, let's go.

If no, may I ask...

what would change your mind?

What would change your mind? Behind that question is the willingness to do something to help them change their mind. People have lots of reasons to not want to join your change—competing priorities, schedule conflicts, focus on specific goals, lack of knowledge of the change goals, limited knowledge of who we are and how we Drive Change, and so on.

The trick to not get stuck with a *no* has two parts:

First, always get your no from the actual person.
Then ask them what it would take to get to yes if..."

There are multiple ways to make something work or learn something new that has not been explored because we limit our options only to a *yes* or a *no*. Encourage the person giving you a "yes, if..." to ask anything of you. If they'll let their mind stretch, they'll usually find you a way to a *yes*.

For example, I once had a senior manager say:

You'll have my *yes* if you can get my peer to say *yes* too, but he never will.

I replied:

Thank you.

I'll go work on that.

Eventually, I got my *yes*.

Remember, your *yes* is important. It will keep you trying and making progress. Your change is about your *yes* much more than their *no*.

Even if you get a *no* from the person and can't get them to engage in a "yes, if…" conversation, you can still remember that a *no* doesn't last forever.

Make an educated guess at what they built the *no* on.

Then you can either act on that foundation or, if it is time-based, set a timer to revisit it. In the meantime, see Tactic 45—Clear the Traffic Jam, and start building a detour.

45

CLEAR THE TRAFFIC JAM

There are no traffic jams on the extra mile.

—*Attributed to Zig Ziglar*

Goal—To get your change moving toward your goals

Status Quo Tactic—Sitting behind a jam of slow or stopped changes blocks your change

Change Tactic—Clear the traffic jam so your change can speed ahead

Why—Because you don't have to live with the traffic jam; you can clear it

Status Quo Tactic—Organizations are full of changes at various points of their journey—just starting, gaining momentum, stalled, stuck and deteriorating, or almost to their destination. Into this arrives your change. You're eager to get started, but you're told:

Not yet.

Wait!

You can't start until...

Organizational leaders have some sense of how much change is too much for the organization. They reveal this sense whenever you suggest a fresh change.

Funny, the idea of too much change is suddenly absent when they have a new idea for a change. Then their timing is:

Now!

You should have started yesterday.

Why aren't you already done?

This is a classic symptom of Driving People.

I know I'm overloaded because I don't have any time to follow another person's orders.

But I assume others can do more because I can always just issue another order.

When faced with this frustrating double standard, change agents like you grow bitter and pull away from their leaders. Their motivation falls, both for their change and for the changes of their leaders.

I've encountered more than a few organizations that had a lot of change going on, but most changes only progressed at a traffic-jam-like crawl. Too many changes were all underway at once along a narrow route of discretionary and compulsory effort.

At least in a real traffic jam, we can rock out to the radio while we wait. In an organizational traffic jam, all you hear is incessant beeping of people joining and leaving the online meetings that fill your days and frustrate your soul.

The worst part of this problem is that it is so easy to fix. On closer inspection, many of these change vehicles are uninhabited and making no progress.

True confession: For four years, I had a recurring meeting on my calendar that I never attended. It was an international meeting, so it was held late at night for me. They had originally invited me when I worked on a special project. My assignment only lasted a few months, and the special project the meeting was for ended a few years later. Yet that meeting lasted on my calendar because I never took action to clear it off. It wasn't technically in my way, but for all who were looking for my availability those four years, it looked like I was busy with those weekly night meetings.

Finally, I removed the meeting from my calendar, and my week now looked much more balanced. This is a silly, extreme example, but I've coached many people who, upon inspection of their calendars, found many similar meetings clogging the flow of their lives and their changes.

- meetings they attend without speaking
- meetings for topics that are no longer relevant to the company's goals
- the classic meetings that could have been e-mails
- meetings that should have been Teams or Slack posts

I'm confident that your organization needs your change or you wouldn't be reading a book like this, hoping to find tactics to help you achieve it. Chances are good, though, that there is not a clear path to victory ahead of you. You face the status quo of an organization clogged with changes and other leaders who always think there is more room on the road for their pet projects.

What can you do? A lot. And it's simpler than you think.

• • •

Change Tactic—You can clear the traffic jam so your change can speed ahead.

Step 1: Help First

Most people want to get started on their change. The thought of not starting your change so you can devote time to someone else's change seems opposite of why you would use this tactic. But helping the other change is your fastest way to your results.

Survey the road ahead of you—all those stalled or stuck changes and all those changes that are moving but are also taking up more road than they deserve. Offer some help.

1. Calendar clean-up. Look for all the meetings and tasks that are clogging your calendar, and cancel those that don't need to be done. You can delegate or share those that someone else is better at doing. You can shrink those tasks you can do yourself and don't need a team for and thus cancel the team meeting. You can leverage new collaboration tools to stay connected without finding time on the calendar. That will help you free up time and headspace, and it will help others too.

2. Change clean-up. Assess your in-flight changes, and allow yourself to stop (either forever or for now) those changes that aren't as essential to your success. Just like it is okay to stop reading a book that isn't interesting, it is okay to stop a change that isn't producing what you'd hoped when you started.

But I started it...

Don't I have to finish it?

No.

You don't have to finish every change you start.

I've started many changes only to realize that the situation has changed.

The effort for results isn't worth it anymore, or maybe now isn't the right time.

The bottom line: It is okay to stop. In fact, it is better to stop than it is to finish just because you started. This will produce a lot of free time and ability to concentrate on your change. At first it can feel disorienting to not have too much to do. The traffic of our organizations is addicting. We'd hardly know what to complain about if all we had to do was our job. We've gotten too used to the stress of too much to do.

3. Road clean-up. The methods we used to create change are antiquated. You can help other changes by establishing some common practices that make it easier to take part productively in changes. These are simple things such as have meeting agendas, publishing meeting minutes, setting Concrete Goals, shrinking the membership list, and creating a collaboration space to capture asynchronous progress. These simple acceleration techniques make the most of any effort put into a change.

Step 2: Stop All New Starts

This requires partnership with others in your organization. If you can stop all starts until you get the changes underway—either off the road, canceled, or flowing again—then releasing more changes only makes matters worse.

This is basic flow theory, and those of you with Lean, Agile, or Theory of Constraints experience are likely screaming:

Yes!

It's obvious!

It's essential!

I agree.

The challenge for you is to advocate for it and role model it.

I will not start my change until we get changes X and Y moving and Z canceled.

Here's what I can do...

How would you like to partner with me to do this too?

Step 3: Spread Driving Change

It will show my age when I say I grew up watching *The Flintstones* reruns. I loved the hilarity of thinking about Fred Flintstone moving his car made of rocks and logs just by moving his feet. That's a good visual for how all our changes should flow in our organizations. They don't move unless we move.

What you'll notice about the stalled changes on the road is that the drivers are sitting in the car sending e-mails to others and wondering why they aren't completing their task to push the car harder. (For now, let's ignore the fact that in too many organizations, the change leader who is Driving People also has their foot on the brake while demanding faster progress.)

Those stalled change drivers aren't out of the car pushing from their door and hoping the next dip in the road will give them some momentum.

We can help them.

We can teach them about Driving Change. We can role model it.

We can learn what they can do with what they have, where they are, and then we can help them work on the change to get it up and running.

As you get more practice Driving Change, you'll find it is very similar to having a knack for fixing cars. You'll see what is wrong and how to fix it much faster than others. They'll value your help if they're willing to accept it.

Warning: They aren't all willing to accept help. In that case, it's best to go around—that's the next step.

Step 4: Build the Detours

This step could take the form of partnering with another part of your organization to help them change while your organization waits. It could take the form of recruiting a separate team of change agents who will build a path to value that circumvents all the typical routes.

Years ago, in the Guiding Coalition, one of our superpowers was finding alternative paths to success than the traditional organizational flows.

Not every change has to flow from executive meeting to director assignment to middle manager tasking to working level dictates to stagnation to failure. We successfully launched minor efforts from the middle that spread among middle managers, building on their discretion (albeit limited sometimes) to determine how their teams delivered value.

This was the route that many successful Agile adoptions found until just a few years ago. When I first started speaking at Agile conferences in 2015, the big question was this:

How will we get the executives to support our Agile implementation?

And now, in 2021, the big controversies are typically about this:

How can we get the executives to stop forcing us to be Agile?

We can get back to creating detours to value if more change agents accept the fact that the road that flows top down is not the fastest path to value. Instead, start from where you are and build with what you have to create value today. Let the executives catch up later when (if) they get out of the traffic—the traffic of their own making.

Warning: When faced with change traffic, we want to blame the people running those broken-down changes that are blocking our paths. I encourage you to fight that desire. Instead, I encourage you toward compassion.

If the change is a car, then most changes those well-meaning project managers are driving are badly designed cars that barely run. For the sake of this example, let's call our project manager Larry. The duct tape and bailing twine of organization—threats that the boss will get angry and a PowerPoint with menacing schedule boxes on Slide 4 that say you're late—holds Larry's car together. His boss assigned him this change, and he expects Larry to mimic the status quo methods. If we were in Larry's shoes, we wouldn't be doing any better. Our choice to Drive Change and take responsibility for the change and all the obstacles, including Larry's change, is all that is moving us along.

Chances are good that when we walk up to Larry's window and knock to offer our help, he will jump, startled. No one helps. They only honk and yell and complain. He doesn't want to be broken down, but he doesn't know how to get going. You can and should help. It will make all the difference to Larry and your organization.

• • •

I had a friend years ago who shut down a lane of the toll road outside Chicago because she had forgotten about the tolls and didn't have any cash. She couldn't move forward. The honking and yelling kept growing, and her tears kept streaming down her face until a man from a few cars back got out of his car, walked forward, knocked on her window, and gave her some cash for the tolls. He had to invest in my friend to get her moving, but his reward was that he got moving. Did he have to do it? No. But he chose to, and he made all the difference that day for her, for him, and for many other drivers. You can be that guy. Pay their toll. Help them make progress. Do it today. The entire group of people in the flow of change will be in your debt.

46

WRITE A NEW RULE

Important issues should be presented in writing.

—Admiral H. G. Rickover, Doing a Job

Goal—Create a structure to enable and sustain a change

Status Quo Tactic—Make assumptions about rules, and let them limit the change

Change Tactic—Find any actual rules, and then change them or write a new rule

Why—Because enabling rules sustains change

Status Quo Tactic—We derail many changes through organizational rules and the assumptions we make about them.

People will say:

> There's a rule that prevents it.

> There's no policy that says I can do that.

Many go off the rules conceptually versus specifically.

> There's a rule somewhere.

Instead of...

> Section 2.4 of Policy S.30 states...

Teams of conscripts meet these claims of rules with resignation.

> I guess we can't do it.

> Let's quit.

The conscripts didn't really want to create the change anyway so if the rule stops them, then they can go back to their jobs. The team rarely tests the truth of vague rule claims.

> Are we sure there's really a rule?

> Couldn't we get the rule changed?

Many assume that if there isn't a rule against it, we would have been doing it already, so there must be a rule against it since we aren't doing it. That logic is circular yet powerful and goes around and around and around.

These assumptions lead to organizations either stopping changes or designing changes around ghost rules, ethereal vapors of preferences and confusions that waft through the organization, stirred up every time anyone tries to change something.

You probably have a specific example of this in your mind. It's so much the status quo that we all seem to have a story or several stories of times that changes stopped because of ghost rules and conscripted indifference.

• • •

Change Tactic—Find any actual rules, and then change them or write new rules.

Rules can be simple memos or complex and detailed policies. The key to a good rule is that we write it down. Once we write it down, we can store it, share it, and find it. You increase the power of your change when, through a written rule, you share the change with the people who must know it and follow it. Problems stay problems when they hide in vague language without reference to anything solid, so writing a new rule provides an anchor for the new behavior.

• • •

Years ago, I wrote a policy for new mothers returning to work who needed accommodations to pump breast milk at work. There had been unwritten rules allowing mothers in office jobs to take time to pump each day. There was no equivalent flexibility for mothers in industrial positions. Our goal in publishing the policy was to grant minimum accommodations to all new mothers in the organization.

To publish the policy, I had to study other policies to match the format. I had to find other industrial policies on the topic to model this one on; there weren't any. To define the policy, I had to learn the key attributes of who must do what to ensure that each new mother had the smoothest path to accessing this new accommodation. Finally, because there were labor agreements, I had to get both management and labor to approve the policy.

When the command published the policy, it was one of my proudest days of my U.S. Navy career. In the years that followed, change agents from other organizations called me for information on our policy. To give them what I didn't have—a template to copy—was an honor.

Choosing to invest your time in writing a new rule—especially rules that blaze new trails to better workplaces—will be one of the greatest investments you can make during your career journey.

RULE QUESTIONS

All change efforts, if you want the change to sustain, should include these four steps in your change plan:

1. Find the applicable rules or policies.

What rule prevents me from doing X?

What instruction tells you to do Y?

When they quote something, immediately seek that source, and check their facts.

Did they cite the rule correctly?

Are they referencing an old version of the instruction and don't know that someone changed the rule?

You will find many surprises when you actually check people's sources.

2. Change or understand the limitations of the applicable rules or policies.

Seek the modification you need to make it read the way you want.

Seek an exception if a full rule change isn't possible.

Write a new rule if one doesn't exist—a rule that will help support and sustain your change.

3. Document and implement the new rules or policies.

Share the new rule or policy in the applicable places so the rule is easy to find.

4. Ensure that a sustaining organization (typically a policy group, business operations lead, or auditing group) will maintain the new rule or policy.

CHANGE TACTICS
FOR ASSESSMENT

47

CHOOSE YOUR MIRROR

I bid him look into the lives of men as though into a mirror,
and from others to take an example for himself.

—*Terence, Adelphoe*

> Goal—Get high-quality, real-time feedback on your change effort
>
> Status Quo Tactic—Assume the change effort is going well, and if not, it's their fault
>
> Change Tactic—Choose a mirror to reflect reality, and assume a problem is yours to fix
>
> Why—Because we can be even better if we're willing to see ourselves as we really are

Status Quo Tactic—Biologically, because our eyes are on the front of our face, we can't see ourselves. We carry this physical inability into our change. To physically see at least a reflection of our full selves, we need a good mirror. To see the actual status of our change efforts, we need a similar mirror—people or measures or both that can show us how we are doing.

The mirror is only the first part of our needs, though, because when we build these mirrors—groups we seek feedback from, measures of our progress—we build something closer to a fun-house mirror than a realistic reflection. We ask people who support us if we are doing a good job. We measure things we can control—number of communications sent— instead of the user-focused measures such as the amount of adoption and satisfaction scores.

Another limitation we suffer from is that we can see more clearly the flaws in others—their slowness in adopting the change, their skill gaps, and more. This leads us to spend a lot of time explaining what's wrong with them and why they are wrong to resist our change. Rather than investing time in improving ourselves and what we are doing, we create more elaborate orders for them to follow or gather more leadership support to force or coerce them to get on board with our change.

Self-blindness and obsession with the flaws in others rarely work for long. We can turn this around.

• • •

Change Tactic—We can't see ourselves clearly, but we can partner with others who can give perspectives on us and our change. In organizations that often push for perfection, seeking weaknesses, gaps, and failures is counter-culture. Yet the path to more success is through honest assessment, not blind hope.

The simplest way to see reality is to seek resisters of your change. Usually they aren't resisting you personally, although it can feel like that, but some gap or overreach in your change upsets them. Seek them out and listen; don't speak. Look for the things you have done or could do to honor their feedback. I'm not encouraging you to design for their preferences or frustrations (see Tactic 31—Design for the Early Majority) but to honor another perspective and what it can teach you.

To go deeper, you can use the Choose Your Mirror Process included here.

• • •

My entire life changed when I stopped fighting the bad feedback, stopped trying to get the senior leader to coerce the troublesome people into obeying me, and stopped Driving People.

I failed my way into discovering Driving Change. I was passionate about implementing the alternative methods in our organization, but I had used my passion as a weapon against others. When I gave up my right to punish others with my change, I found a whole new road to powerful results. My transformation began when I started listening to their honest concerns about the change plan and the role I played in harming them with my change. My transformation was complete when I acted on their concerns and unilaterally disarmed. I vowed to never again force them to change. I put my energy into creatively designing ways to overcome their obstacles and winning them to my change. That made all the difference.[2]

CHOOSE YOUR MIRROR PROCESS

Choose a colleague you think will give you an accurate reflection of yourself, and watch for your patterns, habits, or gaps that are limiting your effectiveness. Ask them to observe you in your interactions together and share your habits and actions with you.

You want to hear them say:

You did X.

Did you intend to do that?

When you find a gap or problem with your change effort, assume there

---

2. For more on my journey from Driving People to Driving Change, see *Everyone Is a Change Agent*, especially Chapter 1.

is something more or different you can do to change the situation. Spend your time asking for feedback from the people you are trying to reach.

What could I do to better partner with you to achieve Change Z?

Then listen, ask follow-up questions, repeat their request back to them, determine what you will do, and commit to it.

I hear you asking for an improved, more intuitive application design.

If I've got that right, I can set up a meeting for you with my user experience designer to better understand your pain points.

Then I will figure out how soon we can schedule the feature changes in our feature backlog.

48

WHILE YOU WERE AWAY

Influence is when you are not the one talking
and yet your words fill the room;
when you are absent
and yet your presence is felt everywhere.

—*TemitOpe Ibrahim*

Goal—The team's behaviors are the same when you are present or absent

Status Quo Tactic—You Drive People so the team's behaviors shift when you are away

Change Tactic—You Drive Change so the team behaves consistently when you're away

Why—Because we can't always be present, and we don't want to always have to be

Status Quo Tactic—Is there a difference in how people behave when you are present and when you aren't? If so, that's your problem, not theirs.

The difference in their behavior is an indicator that you are still Driving People or that they are assuming you are still Driving People, even when you have switched to Driving Change.

Sometimes a team behaves worse when you are absent, making no progress, and spinning in conversations about how others just don't understand.

Sometimes a team behaves better when you are absent, making progress, and taking responsibility for deciding and driving to results.

If you aspire to be the best leader and change agent you can be, these shifts in behavior show something you are doing that is negatively influencing your team either when you are absent or present.

• • •

Change Tactic—If your goal is a high-performing team that is Driving Change when you are present and when you are away, then you need to ensure that you are role modeling Driving Change with your presence and clearing the obstacles for them to Drive Change while you are away.

To achieve the high-performing state where your team thrives even in your absence, you need to leave your ego behind (you aren't the key ingredient) and focus on developing others. Often team members hold back, assuming that the leader wants to be relied on, missed when absent, and focused on all the time. That's what the status quo has taught them, but there is a better way.

You can help them see how much they know, how much they can do, and how much you have faith in them. Ask someone to lead while you are away, or ask for volunteers to lead in your absence. Meet with them before you leave to get their perspective on how they will run the meeting and how they will model Driving Change. Support and encourage them, and the progress they make while you are away will amaze you.

• • •

My son Ted has spina bifida. His spine didn't close in utero, and he has had a life of surgeries and therapies to help him thrive. Ted's condition often requires me to leave work with a moment's notice to be with him for hospitalizations, surgeries, and recovery. Being Ted's mom for 13 years has given me a lot of time to practice ways to make my teams resilient in my absence.

They never cancel meetings when I'm away because I've always partnered with a team member to be my default replacement when I'm out. Teams keep making progress when I'm away because I've used the tactics in this book, especially Tactic 50. And sometimes I get the nicest stories when I return.

Recently, I returned from another week in the hospital with Ted. My colleague said:

You were with me in the meeting.

I could hear what you would say, and I said it.

It made my heart melt. To be as positive a force in our absence as when we're present is what I wish for you and why I've written this book.

PLANNING TO BE AWAY

This tactic has three parts.

Part 1: Set your assumptions.

1. How do people behave when you are present? Are they Driving People or Driving Change? Are they self-motivated or waiting for instructions?
2. How do you think they behave when you are away? What effect do you think the lack of your presence has on them? Describe it in as much detail as possible.

Part 2: Partner with an observer (a member of the team who accepts this temporary role) to watch the behavior while you are away. Do not share your assumptions with the observer. Instead, ask them to observe the behavior of the team related to Driving People or Driving Change and self-motivation or waiting for prompting.

Part 3: Review the observations once you've returned. What did you learn? What will you do differently because of what you've learned?

You can use this tactic for as small an occurrence as missing one meeting or as large as a leave of absence (sabbatical, bonding leave, extended vacation, etc.).

This is a great check of team progress toward autonomy and a check on your effective role modeling of Driving Change.

You may find that people invoke you while you are out.

This is what April would have said.

That is a good intermediate stop on their journey to fully Driving Change. They are using you for encouragement, not compulsion. Ideally, though, you want them to live Driving Change because it is inside of them.

If you find that the team stops while you are absent and can't decide or move forward, you will want to consider how you are enabling them to still want you to Drive People. You'll likely find that your gaps are as subtle as the words you are using.

For more on this topic, read *Leadership Is Language: The Hidden Power of What You Say—and What You Don't* by David Marquet.

MEASURE THE TO:WITH RATIO

If a man's heart is rankling with discord and ill feeling toward
you, you can't win him to your way of thinking
with all the logic in Christendom.
Scolding parents and domineering bosses and husbands and
nagging wives ought to realize that people don't want
to change their minds.
They can't be forced or driven to agree with you or me.
But they may possibly be led...

—Dale Carnegie

Goal—Asses your method for creating change

Status Quo Tactic—Drive people to adopt the change

Change Tactic—Drive the change with your change audience

Why—Because the more you Drive Change, not people, the better your change results are

Status Quo Tactic—The status quo tactic of Driving People is so pervasive that few people question it. The assumption is that there is only one way to create change: force it.

This status quo tactic has perpetuated despite thought leaders telling us for years to do the opposite. Dale Carnegie warned us in 1936. W. Edwards Deming warned us in 1982. Few listened.

Still today, using fear is the status quo to Drive People to adopt a change.

When we are Driving People, we are doing change *to* people. They are the object of our change. Like all objects, we use them for our purposes, elevating our needs above theirs or ignoring their needs entirely.

When you're Driving People, you are doing things like this:

- Creating plans full of orders others should obey
- Threatening people with punishments or removal of benefits (e.g., lose your bonus)
- Escalating disagreements to their managers to get them to force people to obey you

• • •

Change Tactic—Driving Change works to correct this disposition toward fear, first in the change agent leading the change and then in the people involved in the change.

Driving Change—choosing a change for yourself and clearing the obstacle for others to choose it too—allows you and others to thrive together. It eschews fear and division for hope and partnership.

When we are Driving Change, we are doing change *with* people. They are the catalyst for our change. Like all great catalysts, they unlock their power through partnership with us as we elevate our needs and theirs to produce amazing results.

When you're Driving Change, you are doing things like this:

- Creating change plans where you are acting and testing assumptions to learn more
- Approaching people to learn their obstacles and seek their partnership
- Resolving disagreements by seeking to understand their perspective more clearly

Driving Change is powerful, and it becomes an even more powerful tactic when you complement it with many changes led by Driving Change, not people. Organizations that spread Driving Change have what seems to outsiders as a hidden power source that compels change forward in mystical ways.

There's no mysticism or mystery, just Driving Change, a hidden but growing trend in change.

To assess where your organization is in your transition from Driving People to Driving Change, use the To:With Ratio assessment included here. It will easily tell you where you are in your pivot from one to the other.

• • •

Since Driving People is the near universal status quo in most organizations, it can feel overwhelming to be the first to Drive Change, not people. The ratio of To:With will never change until someone Drives Change.

The rate that the ratio changes can speed up if you build a safe place where Driving Change isn't just an approved alternative to Driving People but is actually the new default. This place may be as small as the change you are leading. It can be as large as a major division of a corporation or a major strategic group in a large organization.

Kotter International, a consulting company founded by John Kotter, partners with clients to build guiding coalitions that drive strategic initiatives across organizations through the power of Driving Change—a volunteer army and a belief that you can get many people to have real urgency to achieve a big opportunity together.

In my career, I've repeatedly built islands of Driving Change in seas of Driving People. If you live the Change Agent's Motto (I will do what I can, with what I have, where I am), you'll be able to shift your local To:With ratio. And from that beachhead, you will also tilt the larger To:With ratio.

TO:WITH RATIO ASSESSMENT

The To:With ratio measures the number of changes built on Driving People against the number of changes built on Driving Change.

You build the ratio by listing all changes you handle or the changes that are affecting you.

Next, score each one built on Driving People or Driving Change.

Then total the columns. The result is the To:With ratio.

Here is a sample worksheet.

Title of the Change	Built on Driving People (To)	Built on Driving Change (With)
Change A		X
Change B	X	
Change C	X	
Total	2	1

The To:With ratio is a quick portfolio-level metric to show you how much opportunity you have to improve your change tactics and therefore your results. It's meant as a quick check, an honesty check.

An advanced version of this metric is to complete this worksheet for different levels of the organization—executive leadership, middle management, working level. Most organizations, even if they lean toward *with* at the executive level, skew toward *to* at the middle management level. That skew in ratio can reveal an enormous opportunity to engage middle management and tailor your tactics to their unique needs.

For more thoughts on how this skew causes the middle to be pressured and crushed, see my keynote "The Diamond Layer" at https://tinyurl.com/DiamondLayer

ASSESS TRUST

Trust isn't a byproduct of action; it's an ingredient.

—*April K. Mills*

Goal—Leverage trust to accelerate change
Status Quo Tactic—Once you change, I'll trust you
Change Tactic—Offer trust, and then they'll change
Why—Because trust is foundational to all change

Status Quo Tactic—When you're Driving People, you've built your change on mistrust. If I'm Driving People, I assume you won't adopt the change unless I force you to. I plan your actions for you because I don't think you can figure out how to create the change.

When we roll out a change, we demand that the change audience adopt the change without question, demanding that they trust us and our change plan to be perfect for their situation and timing. We label their lack of immediate, enthusiastic support as resistance. We withhold trust from them until they prove through their blind compliance to our plan that they are onboard with our change.

• • •

Change Tactic—**Trust isn't a byproduct of action; it's an ingredient.** You must build trust into your change in order for it to grow. When we Drive Change, we flip from demanding that people trust us and showing we don't trust them to asking them to trust us by watching our actions. We're asking them to partner with us so we can better trust each other in the future.

Are you struggling to speed up your organizational results and your professional development? To accelerate both requires overcoming a lack of trust between managers and employees. When a manager lacks trust in an employee, they insert reviews, meetings, and approvals to ensure work is accomplished as expected. These empowerment bottlenecks are a tremendous source of frustration and wasted productivity. Once those bottlenecks are inserted, we rarely remove them. The bloat of approvals slows any fast-moving organization to a crawl.

When a manager doesn't trust an employee, the lack of trust lowers employee empowerment because they can't contribute their expertise fully, and confusion, delays, and diminished results abound. We know that when we trust ourselves and each other to work autonomously, we can contribute all our talents and achieve more faster. We know that when teams and individuals self-manage within their level of competency, they innovate faster.

We know that when we increase trust:

1. employees are more motivated, accomplished, and satisfied.
2. managers are more efficient and effective.
3. your organization speeds up.

Everyone wins.

You can use this Competency and Authorization Assessment formally or informally. Having the conversation and aligning where you perceive yourself are the important parts.

Increasing trust is a journey through four authorization tiers.

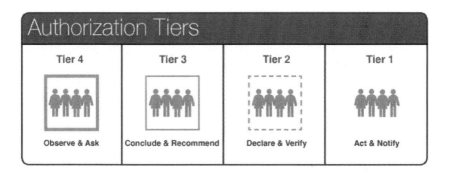

As an employee moves through the four authorization tiers, they may contribute more of their unique talents.

Trust is a two-way street. Employees must earn the trust of their managers. Managers need to communicate clearly what they can trust their employees to do and what the employee must do to increase that trust. Both sides need agreement about where they are, where they are going, and what needs to be done to get to the next tier.

Employees and managers share the responsibility to develop themselves and each other toward Tier 1. When they do, they will act, grow, and speed up the organization.

The Competency and Authorization Assessment included here is a diagnostic designed to speed up the formation, growth, and sustainment of trust between employees and managers. We can use it for trust between change teams and their change audiences too. It draws inspiration from David Marquet's work (*Ladder of Leadership*) and from the U.S. Navy's nuclear power program's lessons learned for creating high-trust relationships and a high-trust organization.

Increasing trust requires managers to have confidence in the employee's ability to execute work within the technical, business, and change contexts. To build more trust, a manager needs to describe clearly an employee's current abilities in three key areas and outline a plan for improving them. When the manager and an employee use the same tool to conduct a self-assessment, they can compare their impressions in a productive dialog. Together they can accurately assess the employee's current skills and agree on a plan that will allow them to build more skill and more trust.

The Competency and Authorization Assessment focuses on three key areas: technical, situational awareness, and change agency.

When you understand the three competencies and four authorization tiers and apply them through the assessment tool, you can have a candid, coherent conversation about building trust and organizational acceleration.

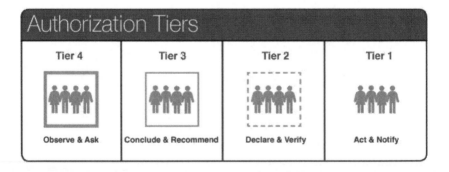

	Tier 4 Observe & Ask	*Tier 3* Conclude & Recommend	*Tier 2* Declare & Verify	*Tier 1* Act & Notify
Employee	Share your observations and ask for direction. Don't hesitate. This is the time to learn quickly and publicly.	Present your conclusions and recommend actions to get approval and help to proceed.	Declare your intent. Expect quick feedback and permission to proceed.	Act, and then notify your manager of what you have done or are doing.
Manager	Ask the employee to reveal skill and knowledge gaps so you can mutually design and enact a learning plan for the employee to proceed to Tier 3.	Identify and close skill and knowledge gaps so the employee can proceed to Tier 2.	Enable the employee to close remaining skill and knowledge gaps so the employee can proceed to Tier 1.	Challenge the employee to continue to expand their skills and knowledge to increase their autonomy and influence.

Technical skills are an obvious expectation.

We focus on ability to do the work without supervision, but we cannot emphasize enough the importance of a willingness to admit the limits of technical knowledge and quickly partner with other experts to speed up innovation or problem resolution. Also, there is an ever increasing need to keep technical skills current to the leading-edge knowledge and methods. We add these technical partnering and continuous learning habits to core technical knowledge to produce a fully technically competent individual. Technical in this sense does not mean just historically technical knowledge (e.g., engineering, manufacturing, operations) but any technical knowledge held by someone in the employee's profession, be that engineering, design, operations, information technology, human resources, legal, or finance.

Situational awareness is a key differentiator in employee performance and crucial knowledge.

It's always essential to know who the key players are in the organization. What this assessment adds is an expectation to maintain a growing network inside and outside the organization to ensure you can sense changes in the markets and technology landscape. Added to this is a growing need for everyone to know the legal, ethical, and technological boundaries of their work. The rapid rate of change inside and outside the organization also requires skill in staying up-to-speed on the latest efforts inside the organization to drive improvements, sales, or strategic shifts.

Change agency is an emerging key competency.

With many people stuck in the status quo, they need a list of "do this, not that" hints to prompt better change agent behavior. As outlined in the Introduction and Appendix 1 and expounded in *Everyone Is a Change Agent,* the Change Agent Essentials are those hints that show anyone in the organization how to Drive Change. The Change Agent Essentials can be the foundation of change competency that all employees need before they attempt to create change today.

Added to the Change Agent Essentials is the ongoing responsibility each person has to keep their manager informed as they act quickly to Drive Change into and throughout the organization.

You can complete the Competency and Authorization Assessment here or download a PDF copy at https://engine-for-change.com/weblog/competency-and-authorization-assessment/

COMPETENCY AND AUTHORIZATION ASSESSMENT

Name:

Date:

Completed by (if not a self-assessment):

Assessment context (project or role):

Competency Scoring

For each competency listed on the assessment, rate yourself (or your employee) as novice, learning, or competent. Here are some phrases to help you decide which of these competency levels apply.

Novice: I have not done this much yet. This is definitely something I could do better.

Learning: I have done this sometimes. I am occasionally trusted to act autonomously, and sometimes I need additional help. It is not foreign to me, but it is certainly not comfortable for me every time.

Competent: I've got this. I am trusted to do this on my own in most situations. My experience has made me very comfortable using this skill.

The ratings are not as important as the discussion that happens when an employee and a manager talk about their assessment of the employee's competence. Together they can identify differences that are causing trust roadblocks and agree on an action plan that will allow the employee to build skills where necessary.

These ratings are a snapshot of current skills measured on the day of the assessment, and they apply to the current work context only. It is normal for people who are completely competent in one context to be novices in many other areas when they accept a new role or a new project with a new team. There is always a learning curve. Helping people effectively and efficiently along that learning curve is what this process is all about.

Authorization Tier Scoring

Once you have evaluated your skills (or your employee's skills), you can score it against the Four Authorization Tiers. The competency assessment describes the current state, so only use it to determine the Current Authorization Tier.

Tier 4: Novice for most skills. This is appropriate when a person joins a new team or starts a new position or project. The goal of Tier 4 is to teach humility and admit the limits of their knowledge and leverage their naïve view to generate innovative ideas for the organization.

Tier 3: Proceed to Tier 3 when you have marked some attributes as Learning. The employee should show competence in the Change Agent

Essentials and basic technical competence, and know when to connect with other technical experts before moving to Tier 2.

Tier 2: Proceed to Tier 2 when you have marked all attributes as Learning or Competent. Do not proceed to Tier 2 if you have marked any attribute as Novice.

Tier 1: Proceed to Tier 1 only when an employee is competent in all skills and shows the humility to continue to look for gaps in their personal knowledge. The employee must mark Competent in all and stay Competent in all to maintain Tier 1.

For the Target Authorization Tier, you can select the tier that is one higher than where the employee is currently. Set a reassessment date soon to ensure a focus on rapid growth up through the tiers.

PROCESS

Pre-Work: Review and Read. Review the Change and Authorization Assessment skills, and read the Introduction, Appendix 1, or *Everyone Is a Change Agent* to familiarize yourself with the Change Agent Essentials.

Step 1: Self-Evaluation. Review the competency attributes. Select your competency level for each attribute: Novice, Learning, Competent.

Use the notes portion to describe why you scored yourself the way you did. Be specific.

Score your assessment, and mark your current Authorization Tier and your target Authorization Tier.

Step 2: Manager Evaluation. (Do this in parallel with the self-evaluation.)

Review the competency attributes for your employee.

Select what you think their competency level is for each attribute: Novice, Learning, Competent.

Use the notes section to describe why you scored them the way you did. Be specific.

Score the assessment, and mark their current Authorization Tier and what you set as their target Authorization Tier.

Step 3: Meet and Discuss. Schedule a one-on-one meeting to discuss the employee's and the manager's assessments and scoring. Start by comparing the current Authorization Tiers, and target Authorization Tiers for overall alignment. Then work through the attributes as necessary to discuss different perspectives and scoring. The goal of this session is to align on the score together, not to prove one or the other wrong. After you've agreed on the assessment, discuss specific actions and opportunities to improve the employee competence to reach the target Authorization Tier.

Step 4: Reassess. Before you end the one-on-one meeting, fill in the "Reassessment by" line at the bottom of the assessment. Make it sooner rather than later to drive urgency to action.

TRUST THE PROCESS

As the employee and manager go through this process, you will build trust in yourself and each other. This will empower you to act with more autonomy to innovate faster. Both the employee and the manager will do more of the work they love and will waste less time with unnecessary meetings.

The employee wins. The manager wins. The organization wins. Trust the process.

ASSESSMENT

Technical Skills	Novice	Learning	Competent
Technically qualified and able to apply technical knowledge to project tasks without oversight			
Partners with and learns from other technical experts to achieve shared goals			
Pursues continuous learning to maintain a thought-leader role in the technical specialty			
Notes:			

Situational Awareness Skills	Novice	Learning	Competent
Knows the organization hierarchy and key players			
Develops a growing network of internal and external contacts to improve sensing of activity, opportunity, and threat			
Understands the system interactions essential to organizational results			
Aware of the legal, ethical, and technological boundaries necessary to ensure safe action			
Maintains effective knowledge of ongoing actions that could be partners or conflicts			
Notes:			

Change Agency Skills	Novice	Learning	Competent
Implements the Change Agent Essentials (from *Everyone Is a Change Agent*)			
Drives Change, not people			

Change Agency Skills	Novice	Learning	Competent
Creates and maintains change buffers			
Sets Concrete Goals			
Maps the terrain: checks for settlers and declares boundaries			
Challenges assumptions			
Focuses on sustainment			
Tries: acts quickly to experiment, learn, and improve			
Communicates actions and results regularly to the manager to maintain the manager's awareness			
Notes:			

Select One	Current Authorization Tier	Select One	Target Authorization Tier
	Tier 4: Observe & Ask		Tier 4: Observe & Ask
	Tier 3: Conclude & Recommend		Tier 3: Conclude & Recommend
	Tier 2: Declare & Verify		Tier 2: Declare & Verify
	Tier 1: Act & Notify		Tier 1: Act & Notify
Notes:			

COMPETENCY-BUILDING ACTION PLAN

Reassessment by:

CONCLUSION

CONCLUSION

The psychological state of Agency causes human progress and the absence of this psychological state causes stagnation.

—*Martin Seligman*

When we began, we knew the odds were against us. Only 1 in 10,000 actually sees a path to somewhere different and acts on that knowledge. Just by getting to the end of this book, you've defied the odds. Once you've acted on one of the change tactics, you'll be in a rare class of exceptional change agents. Stop and celebrate. I won't look while you do your favorite happy dance.

Martin Seligman recently published a paper on "Agency in Greco-Roman Philosophy." His study of agency shows it is both ancient and rare. With efficacy, optimism (including future-mindedness), and imagination, Seligman argues that agency is vital to human progress and that its absence drives stagnation. I wholeheartedly agree. I hope that you agree too.

Through your work—escaping the status quo, Driving Change, and helping others join you—you will transform your life, your work, your community, and more.

The world is longing for change agents like you. With so much change bombarding us and so much more positive change left to do, there's not a moment to lose.

If you haven't changed tactics, start today.

If you've already started, speed up.

I've included another copy of the Change Tactics Scorecard so you can continue to track your practice and progress. Choose which change tactic you will try next.

Only through consistent practice will you grow your confidence and capability. Only through your consistent, visible role modeling will you influence others to choose to Drive Change too.

Remember, when you encounter others Driving People, muster all your compassion toward them. You were once like them. You can help them escape that status quo and choose to Drive Change too.

You are a change agent. It isn't easy, but it isn't hard, either. It's worth it. Continue to defy the odds!

• • •

P.S. Before we part ways, I have a special bonus for you. You can give to any nonprofit the gift of free, licensed PDF versions of both *Everyone Is a Change Agent* and *Change Tactics*.

If you're a leader in the nonprofit, you can connect with me directly or refer the nonprofit leaders to me. Simply e-mail me, or encourage them to e-mail me at april@engine-for-change.com.

The subject line should read: Nonprofit Book Offer. Include the official name of your nonprofit in the e-mail so I know who to list on the PDF license. Together, we can help the world Drive Change.

CHANGE TACTICS SCORECARD

Check your score again.

Tactic	Title	+/-
1	Shift from Forcing to Influencing	
2	Control Your Change	
3	Break Free from the Power Paradox	
4	Replace Certainty with Humbleness	
5	Tell Your Story	
6	Tell Stories about Today	
7	Cultivate Followers at a Distance	
8	Absence Makes the Heart Grow Fonder	
9	Let Them Feel It	
10	Sort the Active from the Passive	
11	Practice Wound Care	
12	Let the Conscripts Leave	
13	Check for Clarity	
14	From Consensus to Commitment	
15	From Helpless to Empowered	
16	Find Your Hidden Change Agents	
17	Study the Hometown Prophets	
18	Build a Team Full of Superheroes	
19	Shine a Light on the Invisible People	

Tactic	Title	+/-
20	Create Your Relay Team	
21	Say Their Names	
22	Pile Up the Partnerships	
23	Build a Tower of Support	
24	Heat Up the Teacup	
25	Shrink the Change	
26	Give It a Title (Not a Name)	
27	Create a Different Future	
28	Speed Up the Pace	
29	From Change Waterfall to Change Agility	
30	A Healthy Dose of Change Design	
31	Design for the Early Majority	
32	Design for Joy	
33	Sketch the System	
34	Calibrate the Change to the Half-Lives	
35	Make the First Step Easy	
36	Scale the Change	
37	Make Stone Soup	
38	From Consumption to Renewal	
39	Create Your Opportunities	
40	Feel the Momentum	
41	Eliminate the Trivial	

Tactic	Title	+/-
42	From Events to Daily Moments	
43	Move the Results into the Meeting	
44	Don't Stall Behind No	
45	Clear the Traffic Jam	
46	Write a New Rule	
47	Choose Your Mirror	
48	While You Were Away	
49	Measure the To:With Ratio	
50	Assess Trust	

APPENDICES

CHANGE AGENT ESSENTIALS

The Change Agent Essentials are
the mechanisms through which a change agent
unlocks and harnesses
the immense power in ourselves,
other individuals and organizations—
power that until now has been hiding in plain sight.

—April K. Mills, Everyone Is a Change Agent

Change Agent Essential #1—Drive Change, Not People
Driving Change is choosing a change for yourself and clearing the obstacles for others to choose it too. We choose this over Driving People—using coercion to compel others to change.

Change Agent Essential #2—Create and Maintain Change Buffers
A Change Buffer is explicit, different thoughts, behaviors, or policies that allow the change agents and the change to vary from the status quo people and environment. Imagine a seawall holding back the waves of Driving People from an island of Driving Change. Change Buffer types include celebration, friendship, leadership, mindset, personal, and policy.

Change Agent Essential #3—Set a Concrete Goal
A Concrete Goal is change attributes summarized into one statement following this pattern:
<Who> will <experience> <what> <where> <when>.

Change Agent Essential #4—Map the Terrain
Two key parts: Checking for Settlers and Drawing Your Boundaries.
Settlers are the people who "live on the land" of your change, whose lives will be affected by it. Settler types include current, missing, past, and downstream.
Drawing your boundaries involves defining clearly what the limits are of your Concrete Goal so others don't assume you are set on world domination or aren't left waiting for you to create a change for them.

Change Agent Essential #5—Challenge Assumptions
Challenging Assumptions includes several tricks to ensure we are honoring other perspectives and challenging our own. Four key challenges to assumptions are assume their perspective is valid, assume we are only seeing a piece of the whole, assume others have positive intentions, and assume responsibility for unintended consequences.

Change Agent Essential #6—Focusing on Sustainment
Focusing on Sustainment includes considering how you will sustain buffers, funding, partners, and systems once the change shifts from the implementation to the sustainment stage.

Change Agent Essential #7—Try
Trying is finding the courage and confidence to act as a change agent, to drive the change you want without waiting for someone else to do something someday.

For more on the Change Agent Essentials,
read *Everyone Is a Change Agent.*

GLOSSARY

AGILE
  a way of managing projects in which work is divided into a series of
  short tasks, with regular breaks to review the work and adapt the
  plans (Oxford)

BEST PEOPLE
  people who are (1) excited about your change and (2) willing to
  Drive Change, not people

BEYOND ACCESSIBLE PLAY
  a design choice to design past the laws that require certain accessible
  features to a playground that exceeds the needs of all children so there
  are truly no barriers to play

CHANGE AGENT ESSENTIAL
  a recommendation for action based on experience and resulting in
  similar situations; a heuristic

CHANGE AGENT'S MOTTO
  I will do what I can, with what I have, where I am.

CHANGE AGILITY
  building cycles of learning about usability and change obstacles into
  the product or process design cycles so we can design the product or
  process for easy use and implementation

CHANGE ALGEBRA
  a description of a change story using variables to substitute for
  specific people, changes, and organizations

CHANGE BUFFER

explicit, different thoughts, behaviors, or policies that allow the change agents and the change to vary from the status quo people and environment

CHANGE PATHS

graph comparing Driving People to Driving Change on an axis of energy to drive the implementation versus distance toward the goal and sustainment

CHANGE SCARS

the psychological vestiges of bad past change efforts that manifest as physical and emotional reactions to fresh change

CHANGE SUFFERING

the physical, emotional, and spiritual pain experienced with poorly implemented change

CHANGE WATERFALL

Where all the change falls onto the organization or customers after all the work of readying for it is complete

CONCRETE GOAL

change goal summarized into one statement following the pattern: <Who> will <experience> <what> <where> <when>

CONSCRIPT

someone forced to join a change against their will

DRIVING CHANGE

choosing a change for yourself and clearing the obstacles for others to choose the change too

DRIVING PEOPLE

using coercion (e.g., orders, fear of negative consequences, removal, or application of positive consequences) to compel others to change

LEARNED HELPLESSNESS
: when experience with uncontrollable events leads to the expectation that future events will elude control and disruptions in motivation, emotion, and learning may occur (Seligman)

ORGANIZATIONAL TIME WARP
: when time runs differently inside versus outside the organization

PLAYACTING
: when an executive only superficially invests in getting the task done versus actually committing to the change

POWER PARADOX
: we assume others are much more powerful than they are, and we assume we are much less powerful than we are; the antidote for the Power Paradox is the Change Agent's Motto

RIGHT PEOPLE
: people who will respond correctly when we drive them to change

SETTLERS
: people who "live on the land" of your change, whose lives you are affecting; settler types include current, missing, past, and downstream

STATUS QUO
: the existing state of affairs (Merriam-Webster) or the cultural library of how things get done here (as defined by John Roberts, my friend and colleague)

TYPE 1 TRANSFORMATION
: low-risk transformation where something may be a significant, irreversible change for us, but many people have done it before, and it operates by known mechanisms (our caterpillar is becoming a butterfly, but we aren't the first caterpillar to become a butterfly)

Type 2 Transformation

path-blazing transformation where what we are attempting is a significant, irreversible change, and we are the first ones to attempt it

APPENDIX 3
SUGGESTED READINGS AND LINKS

*The only people who achieve much are those
who want knowledge so badly
that they seek it while the conditions are still unfavorable.
Favorable conditions never come.*

—C. S. Lewis

SUGGESTED READINGS

L. David Marquet's books will transform how you think about leadership and language.

Turn the Ship Around!

Leadership Is Language

Don Norman's book will help you see the world in fresh, wonderful ways.

The Design of Everyday Things

Martin Seligman's works will transform how you think about how you think.

Learned Helplessness

Learned Optimism

Richard Sheridan's books about joy are both delightful and practical.

Joy, Inc.

Chief Joy Officer

Seth Godin always challenges the status quo, and he wrote "status quo" almost as many times in his book as I did in this book.

Tribes

C. Northcote Parkinson's dry wit is always delightful. You'll learn about Parkinson's law, the law of triviality, and so much more.

Parkinson's Law, and Other Studies in Administration

TemitOpe Ibrahim's book was a beautiful discovery I made while researching this book. For the faithful, it is a heart-changing read.

The Secrets to Your Win

LINKS

To see what superheroes and hometown prophets Driving Change look like, you can watch these videos of the 2010 Guiding Coalition of Puget Sound Naval Shipyard and Intermediate Maintenance Facility (PSNS & IMF), Culture of Continuous Improvement & Diversity Teams.

Part 1 - https://tinyurl.com/2010CCI-D-Part1

Part 2 - https://tinyurl.com/2010CCI-D-Part2

Part 3 - https://tinyurl.com/2010CCI-D-Part3

Part 4 - https://tinyurl.com/2010CCI-D-Part4

Part 5 - https://tinyurl.com/2010CCI-D-Part5

You can also search through the 600+ posts at my blog engine-for-change.com or watch my library of keynote videos at http://www.youtube.com/c/AprilKMills.

APPENDIX 4
REFERENCES AND ENDNOTES

"Abraham Cowley." *Wikiequote*. https://en.wikiquote.org/wiki/Abraham_Cowley

"Agile." *Oxford Learners Dictionary.* https://www.oxfordlearnersdictionaries.com/us/definition/english/agile

"Albert Einstein." *Goodreads.com*. https://www.goodreads.com/quotes/9241778-time-is-relative-its-only-worth-depends-upon-what-we#:~:text=%E2%80%9CTime%20is%20relative%3B%20its%20only%20worth%20depends%20upon%20what%20we,do%20as%20it%20is%20passing.%E2%80%9D

"Albert Schweitzer." *Wikiquote*. https://en.wikiquote.org/wiki/Albert_Schweitzer

"Alice's Adventures in Wonderland." *Wikiquote*. https://en.wikiquote.org/wiki/Alice%27s_Adventures_in_Wonderland

"Andy Warhol." *Wikiquote*. https://en.wikiquote.org/wiki/Andy_Warhol

Argyris, Chris. *Flawed Advice and the Management Trap: How Managers Can Know When They're Getting Good Advice and When They're Not.* New York: Oxford University Press, 2000.

"Brownfield." *Environmental Protection Agency.* https://www.epa.gov/brownfields/overview-epas-brownfields-program#:~:text=A%20brownfield%20is%20a%20property,substance%2C%20pollutant%2C%20or%20contaminant

"Carl Sagan." *Wikiquote*. https://en.wikiquote.org/wiki/Carl_Sagan

Carnegie, Dale. *How to Win Friends and Influence People*. New York: Simon and Schuster, 1936.

Carroll, Lewis. *Alice's Adventures in Wonderland and Through the Looking-Glass*. Racine, WI: Whitman Publishing Company, 1945.

Conner, Daryl. "The Real Story of the Burning Platform." *Conner Partners*. http://www.connerpartners.com/frameworks-and-processes/the-real-story-of-the-burning-platform

Corbridge, Tanner, Jared Jones, Craig Hickman, and Tom Smith. *Propeller: Accelerating Change by Getting Accountability Right*. New York: Portfolio/Penguin, 2019.

Deming, W. Edwards. *Out of the Crisis*. Cambridge, MA: Massachusetts Institute of Technology, Center for Advanced Educational Services, 1982.

Deutschman, Alan. *Change or Die*. New York: Harper Collins, 2007.

"Don Juan (Byron)." *Wikiquote*. https://en.wikiquote.org/wiki/Don_Juan_(Byron)

Gellerman, Saul W. *Management by Motivation*. New York: American Management Association, 1968.

Godin, Seth. *Tribes*. New York: Portfolio, 2008.

Grove, Andy. *Only the Paranoid Survive*. New York: Crown Business, 1999.

"Helmuth von Moltke the Elder." *Wikiquote*. https://en.wikiquote.org/wiki/Helmuth_von_Moltke_the_Elder

Hickman, Adad, and Tonya Fredstrom. "Hope Is the Cornerstone of Performance for Remote Workers." *Gallup*. February 7, 2018. https://www.gallup.com/workplace/236252/hope-cornerstone-performance-remote-workers.aspx

Hood to Coast. Directed by Christoph Baaden and Marcie Hume. 2011. Video.

Ibrahim, TemitOpe in discussion with the author.

"Julius Caesar (play)." *Wikiquote.* https://en.wikiquote.org/wiki/Julius_Caesar_(play)

Kotter, John. *Leading Change.* Boston: Harvard Business School Press, 1996.

Kotter, John P., and Dan S. Cohen. *The Heart of Change.* Boston, MA: Harvard Business Review Press, 2012.

Kotter, John P., and Lorne A. Whitehead. *Buy-In: Saving Your Good Idea from Getting Shot Down.* Boston, MA: Harvard Business Review Press, 2010.

Lencioni, Patrick. 2002. *The Five Dysfunctions of a Team: A Leadership Fable.* San Francisco: Jossey-Bass, 2002.

Lewis, C. S. *The Weight of Glory: And Other Addresses.* San Francisco: Harper San Francisco, 2001.

Linn, Dennis, Sheila Fabricant Linn, and Matthew Linn. *Sleeping with Bread: Holding What Gives You Life.* Chicago: The Wisconsin Providence of the Society of Jesus, 1995.

Malotaux, Niels. "*How Quality Is Assured by Evolutionary Methods.*" *Malotaux.* October 2, 2004. https://www.malotaux.eu/doc.php?id=2

"Managing Organizational Change." *Gartner.* https://www.gartner.com/en/human-resources/insights/organizational-change-management

Mandela, Nelson. "Inaugural Speech." https://www.africa.upenn.edu/Articles_Gen/Inaugural_Speech_17984.html

Marquet, L. David. *Turn the Ship Around!* New York: Portfolio/Penguin, 2012.

Mills, April K. *Everyone Is a Change Agent: A Guide to the Change Agent Essentials.* Oregon: Engine-for-Change Press, 2016.

--------. Videos. https://www.youtube.com/c/AprilKMills

Norman, Don. *The Design of Everyday Things*. Philadelphia: Basic Books, 2013.

Parkinson, C. Northcote. *Parkinson's Law and Other Studies in Administration*. Cambridge, MA.: The Riverside Press, 1957.

Peterson, Christopher, Steven F. Maier, and Martin E. P. Seligman. *Learned Helplessness: A Theory for the Age of Personal Control*. New York: Oxford University Press, 1993.

"Philip Stanhope, 4th Earl of Chesterfield." *Wikiquote*. https://en.wikiquote.org/wiki/Philip_Stanhope,_4th_Earl_of_Chesterfield

Pinchot III, Gifford. *Intrapraneuring*. New York: Harper & Row, Publishers, 1985.

"Ralph Waldo Emerson." *Wikiquote*. https://en.wikiquote.org/wiki/Ralph_Waldo_Emerson

Rickover: The Birth of Nuclear Power. Directed by Michael Pack. 2014. Video

Rickover, H. G. "Doing a Job." Columbia University. 1982. https://govleaders.org/rickover.htm

Rickover, H. G. "The Never-Ending Challenge." Forty-Fourth Annual National Metal Congress, New York. October 29, 1962.

"Robert Burns." *Wikiquote*. https://en.wikiquote.org/wiki/Robert_Burns

Robison, Jennifer. "Making Hope a Business Strategy." *Gallup*. February 12, 2013, https://news.gallup.com/businessjournal/160361/making-hope-business-strategy.aspx

Rogers, Everett M. *Diffusion of Innovation, Fifth Edition*. New York: Simon and Schuster, 2003.

Sehgal, Ellen. "Occupational Mobility and Job Tenure in 1983." *Monthly Labor Review*. October 1984. https://www.bls.gov/opub/mlr/1984/10/art2full.pdf

Seligman, Martin. "Agency in Greco-Roman Philosophy." *The Journal of*

Positive Psychology 16, no. 1, 1–10. doi:10.1080/ 17439760.2020.1832250, https://www.tandfonline.com/doi/full/ 10.1080/17439760.2020.1832250

Seligman, Martin E. P. *Learned Optimism*. New York: Random House, 1990.

"Seth Godin." *AZ Quotes*. https://www.azquotes.com/author/5621-Seth_Godin

Shapiro, Andrea. *Creating Contagious Commitment: Applying the Tipping Point to Organizational Change*. Hillsborough, NC: Strategy Perspective, 2003.

"Talk: Buckminster Fuller." *Wikiquote*. https://en.wikiquote.org/wiki/ Talk:Buckminster_Fuller

"Terence." *Wikiquote*. https://en.wikiquote.org/wiki/Terence

United States Department of Labor, Bureau of Labor Statistics. "Employee Tenure in 2020." September 22, 2020. https://www.bls.gov/news.release/pdf/tenure.pdf

Valentino, Tom. "A Driving Force throughout Human History, Agency Plays Key Role in Positive Psychology." *Psychiatry & Behavioral Health Learning Network*. December 11, 2020. https://www.psychcongress.com/article/driving-force-throughout-human-history-agency-plays-key-role-positive-psychology

"Vaporware." *Wikipedia*. https://en.wikipedia.org/wiki/Vaporware

"Winston Churchill." *Wikiquote*. https://en.wikiquote.org/wiki/ Winston_Churchill

Links and web addresses may have changed since the publication of this book and may no longer be valid.

ABOUT
THE AUTHOR

April K. Mills is an international consultant and author of *Everyone Is a Change Agent* and *Change Tactics*. She was a civilian U.S. Navy nuclear engineer and founded Engine-for-Change. John Kotter praised April's work as pioneering and incorporated it into his 2016 book, *Accelerate*. She has consulted with technology, transportation, and energy companies and is a keynote speaker at global Agile, Lean, Theory of Constraints, program and change management events and more.

Engine-for-Change serves clients who strive to go beyond fads to fundamentals and who yearn to positively plastically deform their company's change culture. Through a blend of leading-edge concepts and tools and timeless strategies and tactics, Engine-for-Change's clients immediately unleash untapped power in themselves, their people, and their companies.

All of April's proceeds from *Everyone Is a Change Agent* and *Change Tac-*

tics support Gully Crest Homestead, a private retreat center in Washington state for families with children with special needs. Gully Crest Homestead with its breathtaking views of Mount Adams, Mount Rainier, and Mount Hood is a rare place of accessible rest in an ever faster changing world.

To accelerate change worldwide, April offers free PDF copies of *Everyone Is a Change Agent* and *Change Tactics* to any nonprofit. To request free, licensed PDF copies, e-mail April at april@engine-for-change.com with the subject Nonprofit Book Offer. Include the name of your nonprofit, a link to your website, and to whom you'd like April to send the copies.

April lives in Washington state with her husband, four children, and a growing menagerie of animals. She believes God gives each of us talent and calls each of us to shine for His glory. She's honored to help you let your light shine. May God bless you today and always.

Contact April through her blog at engine-for-change.com, on Twitter at @engineforchange, or via e-mail at april@engine-for-change.com.

ABOUT
THE ILLUSTRATOR

Sarah Moyle is a creative catalyst and visual storyteller, a role she created for herself at Intel Corporation and as a freelancer. She likes to say she's "been making Intel engineers uncomfortable since 2011" by challenging teams to change the way they think about work. With strategic art, play theory, and targeted facilitation, Sarah taps into the innate creativity inside each of us and guides teams to discover their own creative solutions to business challenges. Some of her favorite tools include LEGO® SERIOUS PLAY®, and graphic facilitation.

As an illustrator, Sarah specializes in Whiteboard Animation videos, strategy maps, and Sketchnotes, and is working on several children's books. She adores sharing her love of art with her two young children, Owen and Mila.

Sarah's passions focus not only on creating art but in bringing art and play into others' lives by drawing, speaking about the importance of play for creativity, and teaching visual workshops. Her favorite thing is creating immersive experiences for others, especially for Halloween. Come October, Sarah's house is an annual (and spooky) art project all its own. To see more of Sarah's creations, visit her website at www.sarahmoyle.com.

DON'T WAIT FOR
SOMEONE SOMEDAY TO DO SOMETHING; START DRIVING YOUR CHANGE TODAY!

You can do more than just try to survive change. You can thrive amidst change when you harness your innate power as a change agent and help others harness their change agent power too.

At Engine-for-Change, we help individuals, organizations, and communities transform themselves and their results through simple tactics grounded in the *Change Agent Essentials.*

Whether you're creating change in a large organization or starting a small project in your community, you are powerful beyond measure if you Drive Change. We can help you shift from Driving People to Driving Change and achieve powerful, sustainable results.

Founder April K. Mills, an engineer-turned-change-evangelist, is an energizing global voice on change agency, change engagement, and accelerating sustainable results. She is the author of *Everyone Is a Change Agent: A Guide to the Change Agent Essentials* and *Change Tactics: 50 Ways Change Agents Boldly Escape the Status Quo.*

April's proceeds from sales of *Everyone Is a Change Agent* and *Change Tac-*

tics support Gully Crest Homestead, a private retreat center for families who have children with special needs. April founded Gully Crest Homestead near Goldendale, Washington, in 2018 because in a world of accelerating change, we all need more accessible rest.

Contact April today at april@engine-for-change.com

INDEX

Made in the USA
Columbia, SC
03 July 2021